MW00596071

"*One Sunday at a Time* is Mark Hart at his best. In this little gem, he shares more than words or stories or sage advice: he shares his very heart, inspiring countless souls along the way. I'm excited to share this book far and wide, trusting that lives, marriages, and families will be abundantly and eternally blessed by it. *One Sunday at a Time* is a gift to anyone who wants the peace that only God can give."

Lino Rulli
Host of *The Catholic Guy* on SiriusXM

"Mark Hart has given us a gift in his newest book *One Sunday at a Time*, a book that is deeply meaningful and yet accessible, no matter where you are in your faith journey. The approach is deep and rich; it is replete with insights from Scripture, the lives of the saints, and the teachings of the Church. The connection between faith living and faith learning is clear and relevant and his tone is warm and conversational. At times deeply poignant, Hart offers wisdom and insights that are timeless. When the Mass has concluded, Hart reminds us that it is then that our work begins—to reach out to a world in need of deep peace and a renewed sense of joy. This book will move hearts and change lives."

Julianne Stanz
Diocese of Green Bay

"I know how much of a difference it makes to prepare for Mass. Switch off your device and start reading *One Sunday at a Time* and you'll see your encounter with our Lord begin to change from this Sunday. Mark Hart has given us a great gift; I highly recommend this accessible and rich work!"

Curtis Martin
Founder of FOCUS

"I can't think of a better way to keep *Bible in a Year* listeners engaged in Sacred Scripture than to study and pray into the rhythm of the weekly Mass readings. And I can't think of a better resource than this little book or a better guide than Mark Hart."

Fr. Mike Schmitz
Host of the *Bible in a Year* podcast

"When I began reading *One Sunday at a Time* to share my thoughts about it, I figured I would share my favorite part. But then week after week, I just couldn't pick a favorite. Each section of every week's writings is obviously well-researched, beautifully written, and well-articulated, with the primary purpose of helping me learn more and grow in faith by reading God's Word. *One Sunday at a Time* is perfect to be read before Mass (or after!), to be read with a spouse and/or children, to help Mass and the Word come alive for us. This book is a perfect combination of history, humor, and heart. I'm grateful it exists to help men, women, and/or families fall deeper in love with our Lord and his Word because I know the truth: a relationship with the Lord through scripture changes lives. You'll love having this unique book on your bookshelf week after week, and you, too, will struggle to find your favorite part."

Jenna Guizar
Founder and creative director
Blessed is She

"Mark Hart uses his biblical expertise to bring hidden gems in scripture to life! It's the perfect combination of prayer, reflection, and education."

Leah Darrow
Founder of Lux Ministries

"If you've always had that sense that you should do more with the Word of God each Sunday but didn't know how, this is the book for you! Mark Hart has written a set of 'spiritual exercises' based on the Sunday readings that are life-transforming!"

John Bergsma
Author of *Bible Basics for Catholics*
and theology professor at Franciscan University of Steubenville

MARK HART

ONE
SUNDAY
at a
TIME

PREPARING YOUR HEART FOR WEEKLY MASS

A COMPANION TO CYCLE A

AVE MARIA PRESS AVE Notre Dame, Indiana

Nihil Obstat: Reverend Monsignor Michael Heintz, PhD
  Censor Librorum

Imprimatur: Most Reverend Kevin C. Rhoades
  Bishop of Fort Wayne–South Bend
  April 6, 2022

Founded in 1865, Ave Maria Press is a ministry of the United States Province of Holy Cross.

www.avemariapress.com

Hardcover: ISBN-13 978-1-64680-170-1

E-book: ISBN-13 978-1-64680-171-8

Cover and text design by Christopher D. Tobin.

Printed and bound in China.

CONTENTS

INTRODUCTION

Our words have power and weight. We can say something that can uplift a heart or tear it down. Our words can encourage, motivate, build, or destroy. The power that our words hold is a reflection of the One who gave us the breath to speak them—they are a reflection of the power of God's Word.

What we speak, powerful as it may seem, will one day pass away. Our words will be forgotten, but God's Word will remain. The Word of God endures forever.

This companion is designed to help you dive more deeply and purposefully into sacred scripture. *One Sunday at a Time* offers reflections based on the Sunday and holy day of obligation readings for Mass. We are offered an intentional cycle of sacred scripture that the Church proclaims at Mass every day during the year. Over the course of three cycles (a three-year period), Catholics hear most of the Bible. But hearing and listening are two different things. We can passively hear something but ignore it. We can hear something and forget it. When we *listen*, however, we take something in. We wrestle with it. We make it a part of who we are and how we live.

One Sunday at a Time is designed to help you listen and remember. The words we hear each Sunday at Mass are powerful. They reveal who God is and the relationship that he shares with us. They recount the stories of those who came before us in faith. The Word is a great love story, poured out onto simple pages for us.

Use this companion to prepare for the readings each Sunday. The calendar dates of the Sundays, holy days of obligation, and other feasts for the most current Liturgical Year A as determined by the United States Conference of Catholic Bishops are available at usccb.org. Every week provides the citations for the readings so you can look them up in your own Bible or online. If you commit to using this companion—if you make the time to read and reflect, even just one Sunday at a time—your life will be blessed and your Mass experience will never be the same.

Included within each Sunday is an opening prayer, some background information about the scriptures for the week, word definitions, facts about the narratives, focused questions for journaling reflection, and a challenge. All of this is written so that you can really "unpack" what God wants to say to you through sacred scripture each week. And don't dismiss the titles for each Sunday. They're meant as quick phrases to help jog your memory throughout the week. Use them as your week's focus—as easy summaries of God's message.

You can use *One Sunday at a Time* as a personal companion on this journey, or you can gather with a group to discuss the readings and background information as a community. Try using it with your family, especially if you are a parent who is often too busy wrangling children during Mass to even have a chance at hearing the Word of God. Maybe you're a minister or priest looking for content to feed your talks and homilies. This is the perfect resource for you, too.

This year, God wants to speak to you through sacred scripture. The Church is inviting us reconsider the simplicity of being spiritually fully present for Mass. This resource will help you make your journey with God one Sunday at a time. Even just once a week, preparing your heart to fully engage at Sunday Mass means you can encounter the Source of all love, whom we know as God. Your journey begins on the pages that follow. It's time to stop overthinking your spiritual life and start living in harmony with the liturgy of the Church. It's time to take it *one Sunday at a time*.

ADVENT

Put on the Armor of Light

First Sunday of Advent

OPENING PRAYER

Lord, your brightness shines within all those who love you. You are my sword and shield. You defeat evil with the light that shines forth from you. Jesus, be my armor. Help me put on the armor of light, that I may be able to fight for you. Amen.

> **First Reading:** Isaiah 2:1–5
> **Responsorial Psalm:** Psalm 122:1–2, 3–4, 4–5, 6–7, 8–9
> **Second Reading:** Romans 13:11–14
> **Gospel:** Matthew 24:37–44

BEYOND WORDS

Darkness has a subtle way of overcoming us. As seasons change—the days shorten, and the nights get longer—the light almost "narrows." The same can be said of the spiritual life. When we give in to selfish wants and desires, sin darkens our lives and intellect. Just as St. Paul is warning the believers in Rome to "cast off the works of darkness" (Rom 13:12) and protect themselves (just as they saw the Roman soldiers do with battle gear) with "the armor of light," so must Christians be aware of the battle between light and darkness raging on around us.

The prophet Isaiah uses this battle language and imagery in the first reading this week, reminding us that it is from the Lord's mountain and house that victory will come. After reminding us of the battle our souls are embroiled in, Christ turns our attention and hearts upward in this gospel from St. Matthew, warning us to be prepared, not only for the battle, but also for its end. The Son of Man will come back at a time beyond our knowledge. The war will subside. Darkness will be cast away. Even in the night—even in these dark times—we must remain spiritually awake and astute. Advent offers us the chance to slowly, weekly, breathe light into darkness. As the season (and new liturgical year) progresses, the days will lengthen. Over the next four weeks, we will look to the house of the Lord and see his light shine brighter and brighter, as the great Judge draws closer.

RELATED FACT

Oftentimes in sacred scripture when we read "the night" or "the darkness," as we do in the second reading from St. Paul, it is intended to have a dual purpose. While the author may be speaking literally about the time of day, when sinful acts such as drunkenness and promiscuity typically happen, it is often meant to convey even more. The "night" and "darkness" are symbolic references to the evil and death that infest and infect the present world. We are called to be lights in this darkness, this culture of sin and death, until such time as the one, true Light returns and vanquishes darkness forever.

BEHIND THE SCENES

Note the wordplay in the gospel when Jesus invokes the tale of Noah. The people in Noah's time were not prepared for the flood. Noah began preparing and building the ark when the skies were still sunny. Christ is warning the people to be prepared, which is one of the central themes not only of Advent, but also of the Christian life. No matter how many people try to "predict" the end times, there is no reason to stress if we are living in right relationship with the Lord. This is one of the reasons that the ark was compared, by the early Church Fathers and so many saints, to the Church:

> The contemporaries of Noah would not believe in his warnings as he was building the Ark, and thus they became frightful examples for all posterity. Christ our God is now building his Church as the Ark of Salvation, and is calling upon all men to enter it. (St. Augustine)

> There is no entering into salvation outside the Church, just as in the time of the Flood there was no salvation outside the Ark which denotes the Church. (St. Thomas Aquinas)

WORD PLAY

The phrase "therefore, stay awake" spoke of Christ's coming on multiple levels. This was not only a historical signal to the fall of Jerusalem in AD 70, but also a reminder of Christ's Second Coming in glory. Additionally, we must have the eyes to see Christ among us and before us in the Eucharist, living a life of sanctity and worthiness before approaching the altar. In the same way, some saints saw Advent celebrating the threefold coming of Christ in the manger, at the end of time, and upon the altar.

JOURNAL

1. What battle are you fighting right now? Is it a battle against sin? A fight with a spouse? A disagreement with extended family or coworkers? In what ways is God calling you to ask for his help?

2. If Jesus were to come again right now, would you be ready?

3. What is something in your life that you must get rid of in order to be ready for Jesus's Second Coming? How can you get rid of it?

4. What is the armor of light? How can you use it to fight off sin and evil?

CHALLENGE FOR THE WEEK

This week St. Paul, in the second reading, asked you to put on the armor of light to fight off sin and evil. One piece of the armor is the Rosary. St. Padre Pio referred to the Rosary as a spiritual weapon. Pray the Rosary (or a decade) every day this week. As you pray, really focus on how God will deliver you from the battle you are in.

Knowledge of the Lord

Second Sunday of Advent

OPENING PRAYER

Come, Holy Spirit. Give me the grace to trust the Lord's promises and the courage to cooperate with his will. Father, I surrender to you all of my fears, doubts, and insecurities so that I can serve you to the best of my ability. Open my heart as I dive into your Word so that I may realize how good and faithful you are. Amen.

> **First Reading:** Isaiah 11:1–10
> **Responsorial Psalm:** Psalm 72:1–2, 7–8, 12–13, 17
> **Second Reading:** Romans 15:4–9
> **Gospel:** Matthew 3:1–12

BEYOND WORDS

Prophecy is a tricky thing. Far more than some kind of divinely inspired "fortune telling," the prophets were ordinary people called to share extraordinary things. Many of the prophecies that God entrusted to his holy mouthpieces were speaking of truths both in the present and for the future. The words from today's first reading, however, demonstrate a promise God makes and communicates through Isaiah that would take a long time to come to fruition—centuries, in fact.

God may not act on our timeline, but he does act. Our heavenly Father may not fulfill all of his promises during your lifetime, but he will fulfill them. This is why St. Paul can write with such certainty in the second reading to the Romans. God's holy Word is supposed to bring us encouragement and foster endurance for this Christian walk we are living. Just as John the Baptist pointed us ahead to Jesus's arrival and our ultimate judgment, so the Church echoes our need to spread and share the Gospel with any and all we encounter so that, indeed, the world "shall be full of the knowledge of the Lord"

(Is 11:9). His prophecies might take time to unfold, but that time allows the rest of us to share the Good News with even more souls before Christ returns.

RELATED FACT

As you hear Isaiah say that the "child shall put his hand on the adder's den. They shall not hurt or destroy" (Is 11:8–9), you may be a little confused. Why is some baby hanging out in an adder's (a small poisonous snake) den to begin with? Some scholars have noted that, when in the darkness of their den, a cobra's eyes are wide and sparkle from the exterior light. Such a sight would entice a child to reach in. The verse is intended to imply that when the Messiah comes no harm from a serpent will come to a child. We, the children of God, will have nothing more to fear of the great serpent, Satan, that seeks to destroy us when we are in Christ.

BEHIND THE SCENES

Anyone remotely versed in the Old Testament knows well the importance of the Jordan River. It was where Abram and Lot parted company, where Jacob/Israel wrestled with God, and it was through the Jordan that the wandering Israelites would take Jericho en route to securing the Promised Land. What many do not realize, however, is that this gospel story of a prophetic calling and empowerment beside a river echoes a scene with the prophet Ezekiel. He was commissioned by God beside the River Chebar where there was also a heavenly vision, the voice of God, and a spiritual reception (see Ezekiel 1:1, 2:1–2). Jesus is the new Ezekiel, being sent as a new voice and prophet to the new Israel in a way old Israel (and those familiar with its history) would have recognized.

WORD PLAY

When you read St. Matthew's gospel (as we will all year, now that we are in Cycle A), you'll notice the phrase "kingdom of heaven" proclaimed quite a bit. In fact, if one were looking for the signature phrase the Holy Spirit poured through St. Matthew's gospel, this would be it. Matthew uses "kingdom of heaven" more than thirty times in his twenty-eight chapters. The phrase is far too deep to unpack here, but it might help to think of the "kingdom of heaven" as the kingdom of God being established on Earth. The goal of the Church is to establish and fulfill the will of God on Earth "as it is in heaven."

JOURNAL

1. Do you regularly invite the Holy Spirit into your life? What spiritual gift do you particularly need right now?

2. Is there an area of your life that you haven't given to the Lord? Why? Are you afraid that he won't take care of it?

3. Who is God calling you to share the Good News with? How can you improve your relationship with that person in order to improve their relationship with Christ?

4. What does hope mean to you? Why is it an important part of the Christian faith?

CHALLENGE FOR THE WEEK

Try to see this week through the lens of hope. Hope helps us recognize and give thanks for the good parts of our day, while providing consolation through the bad parts. Although some promises take longer than others to fulfill, hope allows us to realize how present God is in our lives. He is constantly working in our waiting.

Say *Yes* to God

Solemnity of the Immaculate Conception

OPENING PRAYER

Lord, I give you thanks and praise this day for the gift of free will. You have offered us this great gift out of your great love for us. I pray that, through your grace, I may learn how to use this gift in a way that gives honor to you. You know my greatest need, Lord. Please help me to choose it. Amen.

> **First Reading:** Genesis 3:9–15, 20
> **Responsorial Psalm:** Psalm 98:1, 2–3, 3–4
> **Second Reading:** Ephesians 1:3–6, 11–12
> **Gospel:** Luke 1:26–38

BEYOND WORDS

Sometimes we say yes to something without any idea of the consequences or rewards that it will bring. What might seem like a simple "Yes, I can help you move" can turn into a full-day (or even weekend) commitment. "Yes, let's stay out late" can lead to trouble (and a rough morning). Other times we say yes to a service project and find out that we seemingly receive much more than we give. Our ability to make decisions is powerful and can have far-reaching impacts (both good and bad).

This week's readings are about choices and the far-reaching impact they can have. In the beginning of human history, two people made a choice. These people—Adam and Eve—chose to disobey God rather than listen. Just before this reading in Genesis, we see Adam and Eve encounter a spiritual being who convinces them that God's will for them is not good. They believe it and choose to follow their own will rather than stay in a relationship with God. Because humanity disobeyed God and refused to follow God's law, death became a reality and their "yes" to this disobedience created havoc in its aftermath: we were separated from God and our relationship was broken.

In the gospel we hear about another encounter a woman has with a spiritual being. But, this time, the outcome is different. God invites this woman, Mary, to be obedient to his will so that God can undo what our sin has done. Mary says yes to becoming the mother of Jesus, and her consent has far-reaching consequences. In this moment, the world changes. God becomes human and begins his mission of salvation.

Two situations, two choices—one brings death and one brings life. We are given Mary as a model and example of what it looks like to respond to God's will in a way that brings life. God wants to do great things through our lives—and St. Paul reminds the Ephesians of this in the second reading. God wants us to be holy and has chosen us to be a part of his family. We have the choice to respond in obedience and to experience the great things God has in store, or to refuse and to accept the consequences of separation.

RELATED FACT

The archangel Gabriel appears three times in the Bible in both the Old and New Testaments. In the Old Testament, he appears to the prophet Daniel to explain visions. In the New Testament, Gabriel appears to Zechariah (the father of John the Baptist) and to Mary.

BEHIND THE SCENES

The greeting that the archangel Gabriel uses for Mary is unique. The word that we translate into "full of grace" is only found in this single place in the New Testament. It is not a greeting used in the Old Testament in the same way it is applied to Mary. It makes sense, then, that Mary would have been, in some way, "troubled" by what was said and wondered what this greeting meant. Mary would've been familiar with stories involving angelic beings often bringing with them a major message or mission. Standing face-to-face with Gabriel would have been intimidating, to say the least.

Mary's response to Gabriel's declaration of her conception of Jesus seems to mirror the same exchange that Gabriel has with Zechariah earlier in the Gospel of Luke, but the results are different because the disposition of heart was different. Zechariah also questions how his wife might conceive, but instead of receiving an explanation, he loses his voice. The request came from a place of doubt rather than a place of inquisitive trust. Mary's request for clarification prompts Gabriel to explain the role of the Holy Spirit so that she (and all of us) can understand the divine action that is taking place here of God's initiative—not the action of any other event.

WORD PLAY

The response of Mary is to say, "Let it be to me according to your word" (Lk 1:38). This is commonly referred to as "Mary's *fiat*," because the words "be done" are translated from the Latin verb *fiat*. The word also appears in the Lord's Prayer and during Jesus's agony in the garden.

JOURNAL

1. Where are you currently living outside of God's commandments or laws? Are there areas where you are not following God's will? Why?

2. In what ways is God inviting you into something great? How does God want to use your "yes" to do more in your life?

3. What "great things" do you think God might want to do in your life? Where are there unrealized passions and dreams in your adult life? Have you given up on them? Explain.

CHALLENGE FOR THE WEEK

This week, go to the Sacrament of Reconciliation. We all step outside of God's law for our lives sometimes and refuse to be obedient to his will, choosing our own above his. The Sacrament of Reconciliation gives us the opportunity to restore our relationship—it is saying yes to living in God's will and allowing God to do great things in us.

Rejoice in the Lord

Third Sunday of Advent

OPENING PRAYER

Jesus, you bring joy to others. Without you, there is no joy and only emptiness. I have suffered, but you have suffered more. You have willingly suffered for me, and I praise you. Help me know that this life is not a vacation but a pilgrimage. Therefore, I offer any bump in the road to you with a peaceful heart. In this time of preparation for your coming, help me be open to you. Amen.

> **First Reading:** Isaiah 35:1–6a, 10
> **Responsorial Psalm:** Psalm 146:6–7, 8–9, 9–10
> **Second Reading:** James 5:7–10
> **Gospel:** Matthew 11:2–11

BEYOND WORDS

Life will have hardships and sufferings. There will be good times but also bad ones. There will be seasons of joy but also seasons and times of suffering.

How's that for a happy thought? It's encouraging, right? No matter how hard you pray or work to live the right way, bad times will come from time to time. So, why then would the Church tell us to "rejoice" today? Rejoicing in suffering seems to go against common sense, doesn't it?

Isaiah gives us a clue in the first reading, reminding us that flowers will bloom even in the desert. Joy and gladness will overpower mourning and sadness. We have a God who knows your needs and hears your cries and who *responds*! This is cause for great celebration. When we cry out to God, begging him, "Lord, come and save us!" we have a Father who responds. St. James gives us three secrets to keeping this perspective of hope and rejoicing in the midst of suffering: be patient, be firm, and be positive. What a glorious gift St. John the

Baptist received while suffering in prison. It was confirmed that God was working miracles and fulfilling the prophecy of a Messiah. In the midst of personal pain, all hope was restored, for God had come to save St. John and us! Age after age, God's people have called out, sent the SOS signal, waved the white flag, prayed for a deliverer, and, when the time came, they were sent a Redeemer who, through suffering, would restore all hope and save us all. What a reason to rejoice!

RELATED FACT

Phrases like "the glory of Lebanon shall be given to it, the majesty of Carmel and Sharon" (Is 35:2), are lost on most twenty-first-century readers. At the time, the "glory of Lebanon" referred to the majestic cedar trees that bloomed there. They were tall, strong, and seemingly unbreakable. Carmel was known for its great beauty, and Sharon was a region known for its bounty and fertility. Isaiah is telling people who knew the region well that when the messiah comes, the desert will cease to be a wasteland and, instead, become majestic and beautiful and bountiful.

BEHIND THE SCENES

We talk often about how the Lord Jesus fulfills prophecies. John the Baptist is obviously well versed (no pun intended) in the prophecies from the ages that preceded him. So, in the gospel when he asks the question regarding Jesus's identity and fulfillment as the long-awaited Messiah, Jesus points back to Isaiah (which we heard in the first reading) as a way of pointing to himself as the fulfillment. Note that Jesus doesn't say that "the blind *will* see" or "the deaf *will* hear" but, rather, speaks in the present tense: "The blind receive their sight and the lame walk, lepers are cleansed and the deaf hear, and the dead are raised up, and the poor have the good news preached to them" (Mt 11:5). Christ is stating the facts without being self-congratulatory or self-referential. That is one humble Savior.

WORD PLAY

The first reading says that our God comes with *vindication*, which is an interesting word choice. From the Latin *vindicare* meaning "claimed or avenged," the word conjures up the image of a God coming to claim what is rightfully his—namely, his children. As the reading asserts, "He will come and save you" (Is 35:4).

JOURNAL

1. Jesus asks us to be joyful in the midst of suffering. The best example we have of this is the crucifix—Jesus on the Cross. How is God calling you to imitate his willingness to be joyful in suffering?

2. In the psalm for the week, we learn that God gives sight to the blind. Sometimes in our suffering, we can be blind to the good that God is actually doing. Think of a time when you suffered. What good came out of it?

3. In this time of Advent, we are called to prepare for the Savior's coming. How can you prepare with joy?

4. Joy radiates. When we are joyful, others see this and crave the same joy. How can you spread your joy to others? Where do you serve others? What are some simple things you (and your family) can do to really serve this week?

CHALLENGE FOR THE WEEK

When people ask why God would allow suffering, we look to the Cross. Jesus's suffering set us free. Go to your nearest chapel, sometime this week, and meditate on the crucifix. Even if you just stare at it, think of the love that it presents. Ask God how you can imitate him in his suffering.

God Is with Us

Fourth Sunday of Advent

OPENING PRAYER

Lord Jesus Christ, sometimes life is hard, and I feel as if you've forgotten me. Sometimes, I forget you and abandon my prayer life. I thank you for reminding me that you are Emmanuel, and you are always with me. I thank you for the gift of the Eucharist. This Sunday, help me to receive the Eucharist fully aware that your desire to be with me is so strong that you are willing to offer yourself under the appearance of simple bread. As I consume you, I pray that love for you will consume my heart, O God. Amen.

> **First Reading:** Isaiah 7:10–14
> **Responsorial Psalm:** Psalm 24:1–2, 3–4, 5–6
> **Second Reading:** Romans 1:1–7
> **Gospel:** Matthew 1:18–24

BEYOND WORDS

Imagine how challenging it must have been for people in the Old Testament to envision when and where Jesus would come. They knew God promised to send us a messiah to save us. They heard random prophecies spread out over decades and centuries giving them "clues" about where he would be born, what he would be called, and what he would be "like." But piecing it all together would have been really difficult to wrap their heads around. God was seemingly distant, not up close and personal—as though he was not for average people. What would God look like? How would he handle the Romans persecuting his children, the Israelites? How would our one God demonstrate his power over the Romans' "many gods"? And when on Earth was all this going to happen? The people had prayed for Emmanuel to come for (only) thousands of years at this point; when was it finally going to happen? When would God actually "be with us"?

Isaiah gave us some hints and foreshadowing of what to look for: the distant would draw near, through a virgin, and be called "Emmanuel." St. Paul speaks of the power established and seen in the Son of God, who conquered death; these are images that would've resonated with the Christians in Rome accustomed to the "power" of the Roman army bringing not freedom but oppression.

Yes, how confused people must have been to receive this mighty King, robed not in regal linens but swaddling clothes, and placed upon a throne of splintered wood in a common feed box. Emmanuel came in the least likely of manners but fulfilling details God had set in motion hundreds of years earlier. The seemingly distant God drew near, and heaven came to Earth—not merely to "save us" but because of his great desire to "be with us," for he truly is Emmanuel. When we invite him to come and dwell in the manger of our hearts, he (still) does just that.

RELATED FACT

Not once, not twice, but *three separate times* (see Matthew 1:20; 2:13; 2:19) St. Joseph is visited by angels in his dreams—and those are only the instances we know about, straight from St. Matthew's gospel. God can communicate his plan to us in a variety of different ways. So, the next time you're falling asleep in class or dozing at work, feel free to let your teacher or boss know you're not sleeping; you're praying a "St. Joseph's meditation."

BEHIND THE SCENES

Many people reading this passage from today's gospel wonder why our Lord isn't named *Emmanuel* rather than Jesus, if the prophecy quoted from Isaiah is true. Yet, during Advent, we don't pray, "O come, O come, Jesus," but, rather, "Emmanuel." The name *Emmanuel* means "God is with us." The name *Jesus* is a Hebrew derivative of Yeshua/Joshua, meaning "God saves." So why do we defer to the latter?

15

In this case, it's a translation and cultural idiom. "They shall *call his name* Emmanuel" refers more to a nickname or title than an actual "name." For instance, Lebron James has been called "the King" or "King James" by many fans, marketers, and the media. He is not literally a king, though his name indicates that he "reigns" on the basketball court. We are to infer something about his skill and dominance when we hear the title, but not use it as his official identifier. Similarly, *Emmanuel* is a title and designation for Christ, though not his actual "handle."

It's also worthy of mention that the Holy Spirit almost "bookends" St. Matthew's gospel with this notion. In chapter 1, as seen here, we are told the Lord is "God with us," and the very last words of this same gospel—from Christ himself—are "lo, I am with you always, to the close of the age" (Mt 28:20).

WORD PLAY

The term *betrothal* has often confused people over the centuries who are unfamiliar with the marital "process" in the time of Christ. Often confusing it with a mere "engagement," people mistakenly think *betrothal* means the couple is not yet married. The truth, however, is that the couple is married, just not yet living together. In ancient Judaism there was a period of waiting between the time of the marriage covenant and the time of cohabitation/consummation. Typically lasting less than a year, it was a sacred time of preparation for spouses (spiritually) and their future living space (physically). Couples were absolutely seen as married during the betrothal time, and the marriage could only be terminated by death or (in drastic cases) divorce. (For more on the entire marriage process of ancient Judaism, see the Behind the Scenes section for the Thirty-Second Sunday in Ordinary Time.)

JOURNAL

1. Mary and Joseph were not expecting to become the parents of the Son of God. Can you think of a time in your life when God did something unexpected, but it turned out better than you originally planned? What can this experience teach you currently?

2. When Joseph awoke from his sleep, he immediately did what God had asked him to do. Is God asking you to do something that you've been hesitant to do? Be honest with yourself. What has held you back?

3. Do you remember that Jesus desires to save you from your sins? Or do you often hide from God, mistakenly thinking that he could never forgive your sins?

4. Is it hard for you to remember that God is always with you? Why? What can you do to fix that issue?

CHALLENGE FOR THE WEEK

If you don't normally attend Mass during the week, commit to going to daily Mass at least once this week. If you normally attend daily Mass, get there early or stay late to spend time in prayer thanking God for the Eucharist and giving him permission to change you from the inside out.

CHRISTMAS

And the Word Became Flesh

Solemnity of the Nativity of the Lord

OPENING PRAYER

Lord, I believe your light casts out the darkness of sin. No matter how strong that darkness, your light conquers it. Help me, Lord, to see your light and your promise in the Christ child this Christmas. Make my heart awestruck at the humble and loving way you chose to bring our deliverer into the world to bring us back to you. In Jesus's name we pray. Amen.

> **(Mass during the Day)**
> **First Reading:** Isaiah 52:7–10
> **Responsorial Psalm:** Psalm 98:1, 2–3, 3–4, 5–6
> **Second Reading:** Hebrews 1:1–6
> **Gospel:** John 1:1–18

BEYOND WORDS

Existing within every epic movie is a story about two sides—light and dark—at war with each other. The story of good and evil is as old as human history. It is a part of our human condition and experience, and these epic movies follow the same pattern: We meet the heroes and the villains, we see the conflict start, all hope seems lost for the heroes, but in the end good triumphs. There is victory.

We can lose sight of the weight of the Nativity of Jesus Christ and the power this moment still has for us today. For the Jewish people, it was a dark moment. For the past several hundred years, they went from having a thriving kingdom to becoming slaves under new rulers. In the time of Christ, they lived with some relative "freedoms" under the Roman government, but it was a far cry from the kingdom they once ruled. Not only that, but God used to speak to them through prophets, and lately few (if any) voices were heard speaking on behalf of God.

20

Then the moment of Jesus's birth happens, and the tide changes. Looking back on these events, the writer of the Letter to the Hebrews reflects in the second reading about how God, through Jesus Christ, spoke to us in an incredibly intimate way. Instead of using prophets, God himself speaks. God is being clear with us in this moment. God is entering the battle.

At the moment of Jesus's birth, the world seemed filled with darkness, but now there is light. The gospel for Christmas Day begins with an ancient hymn to Jesus. It talks about Jesus, the Divine Word of God, being present at the moment of creation. The gospel writer, St. John, goes on to share about how Jesus is a Light that darkness cannot overcome. Not only that, but Jesus is God literally living with us and among us. God didn't stand outside of the battle; God came to win the war. Christmas is a moment of victory—God's victory—and the incredible gift we are offered to be able to stand alongside Jesus in the light and to claim that victory as our own.

RELATED FACT

The second reading speaks about the relationship Jesus shares with the angels in heaven—namely, that Jesus is superior to the angels and that all of the angels worship him. Traditionally, there are considered to be nine "choirs" or levels of angels: angels, seraphim, cherubim, thrones, dominions, virtues, powers, archangels, and principalities.

BEHIND THE SCENES

The gospel reading focuses on Jesus as "the Word" that was present with God at creation and through which all of creation happened. It is speculated that this may be one of the oldest Christian hymns in existence. St. John was intentional about putting this at the beginning of his gospel. While Matthew and Luke focus on the birth of Jesus, John points to the divine origin of Christ. This hymn calls back to the Old Testament scripture—the story of creation where God speaks "the Word" and the world is created.

21

The idea of a divine "word" (or *logos* in Greek) was present in both Greek and Jewish philosophy before the time of Christ. For the Greeks, the *logos* represented the universal principle that animated and ruled the world. Some Greek philosophers, called Stoics, saw the *logos* personified in their various gods.

Within early Jewish philosophy, the *logos* was the creative Word of God, the revealer of God (similar to an angel), and occasionally it even borrowed from the Greek philosophy of the day that saw the *logos* as the bond that held the world together.

St. John saw value in these ideas but saw them as incomplete. The *logos* was not simply a word from God, but God himself, and Jesus Christ was the Word through which all the world was created and the Light that holds human life together. It is a good example of how often philosophy or reason can help point us in the right direction, but sometimes they require the lens of faith in order to help them reach their full potential. In the case of the Greek and Jewish philosophers, they had an understanding of a concept, but needed the revelation of Christ to understand that what they were actually speaking about was a person.

WORD PLAY

The first reading mentions *sentinels* that herald God's salvation. Sentinels were watchmen who stood guard over the Temple and would have been the first to catch sight of a messenger coming through the mountains. The image the prophet Isaiah is painting is of these watchmen standing on the walls of the ruined Temple, still guarding it, as they see God coming to restore what has been broken.

JOURNAL

1. Christmas can be a time of great joy, but for some people it's a time of sadness as we remember loved ones who are not with us. The first reading says, "The LORD comforts his people" (Is 52:9). Where do you need God's comfort and peace this holiday season?

2. Where in your life has God won a victory? Recall the good things God has done for you today and write them down.

3. Have you seen God shine light into the darkness of the world recently? Where? How can you be a light in dark times to others?

CHALLENGE FOR THE WEEK

Jesus Christ is the Light that shines in the darkness and the "light of the human race." We can share that Light with others. Over the Christmas season, commit to three things that will allow you to be a light to others, especially in your own home. Think about your actions, words, and intentions as you move through the coming month, and resolve to serve out of love, speak in a way that builds people up, and think well of people rather than allow negativity to drive your attitude.

Thy Will Be Done

Feast of the Holy Family

OPENING PRAYER

Jesus, your every action on this Earth was for my good, culminating in your death on the Cross to save us from our sins. You exhibit the way of perfect love. Through the virtuous example of your Holy Family, teach me to strive toward holiness, not perfection. Amen.

> **First Reading:** Sirach 3:2–6, 12–14
> **Responsorial Psalm:** Psalm 128:1–2, 3, 4–5
> **Second Reading:** Colossians 3:12–21
> **Gospel:** Matthew 2:13–15, 19–23

BEYOND WORDS

This is the time of year that our homes begin to fill with Christmas cards that show us perfect images of families and friends. However, Christmas cards meant to spread the holiday spirit can leave some families feeling like they don't measure up. Then, as the Christmas season moves on we come to this week's liturgical celebration, which can threaten the same.

It can be spiritually challenging on a feast day such as this one to look at our own families and compare ourselves to the holy family of Nazareth. But no family can compare to their perfection. There was the Blessed Virgin who never sinned; St. Joseph, the man God deemed fit to raise his only son; and of course, the Second Person of the Holy Trinity, God incarnate, as the child. It's in this moment that we are wise to consider, again, the title of today's feast: it is not known as the Feast of the perfect family but, rather, of the Holy Family. While we are never going to be perfect families we are still called and able (by the grace of God) to be holy.

When we turn to the readings, we are given profoundly simple yet practical advice as to how we become truly holy. In the gospel, we

find St. Joseph asleep and dreaming. In these dreams, an angel speaks to Joseph and Joseph listens and obeys. What made St. Joseph such a model of humility and virtue is how he trusted the Lord and obeyed him when told to take the family and flee to a foreign country. Joseph assuredly would have been distressed, but he went and, in doing so, demonstrated his profound trust in God. We see in this image St. Joseph not solely as a father but as a son of the Heavenly Father.

Holiness is achievable by the grace of God, it's just not easy. When we allow ourselves in small every day ways to hear the voice of God and to follow his commands, we will grow in holiness. When we strive for virtue even in the face of hardships and doubts, we become more like our blessed mother and St. Joseph.

RELATED FACT
There are several instances in the Old Testament when people fled to Egypt in search of safety. The holy family are in Egypt because Jesus is going to relive the exodus experience of Israel and to do so, he, too, must "come out of Egypt" and return to the promised land.

BEHIND THE SCENES
St. Joseph is a righteous man and guardian of the Church. Scripturally speaking, however, we don't really know much about him. Outside of his trade as a carpenter and his brief appearances in the gospel infancy narratives, the gospels are fairly silent about him. By the time Jesus comes onto the scene as an adult and begins his public ministry, there is no mention of him. Even at Jesus's first recorded sign at the wedding feast at Cana, we are told Mary is there with Jesus and his companions but there is no mention of Mary's husband, likely intimating that Joseph had already passed away by that point.

WORD PLAY
The second reading from St. Paul's letter to the Colossians bids that wives be "subordinate" to their husbands. The word *subordinate* means "under the ordained/order" or "under the mission." A closer examination of this text reveals that husband and wife have separate

but complimentary roles: the call of the husband is to suffer and die, offering his life in service of his wife the way Christ did upon the cross for the Church, while the wife's role is to live "under" that calling and allow her husband to die in this way, dying to herself in the process. This verse is a call to selfless love, first, on the part of the husband and correspondingly on the part of the wife.

JOURNAL

1. What is one small way you can change your life this week to strive for virtue and grow in holiness?

2. Think about the ways in which your family shows their love for one another through their actions, words, and priorities. How is love expressed for each unique member of your family?

3. Reread Colossians 3:15–17 and take note of the word or phrase that sticks out to you. What does it mean? What is Jesus saying to you through this word or phrase?

CHALLENGE FOR THE WEEK

This week, identify a friend or family member who gives their love selflessly. Find a concrete way to express your love to that person, whether it is by doing the dishes without being asked, or sharing a note of honest affirmation and gratitude.

She Kept All These Things
Solemnity of Mary, Mother of God

OPENING PRAYER

Oh, Blessed Virgin Mary, I humbly ask for your intercession today as I reflect on God's Word. As my mother, I know you desire what's best for me and are committed to helping me grow in holiness. Just as the Holy Spirit overshadowed you, I pray the Holy Spirit would come upon me so that I could be inspired to see God's goodness. Amen.

> **First Reading:** Numbers 6:22–27
> **Responsorial Psalm:** Psalm 67:2–3, 5, 6, 8
> **Second Reading:** Galatians 4:4–7
> **Gospel:** Luke 2:16–21

BEYOND WORDS

We learn a lot from our parents, and for many of us our mothers played a critical role in making us the people we have become. For young children, a mother is literally a source of life. Moms teach first words, catch us when we fall, and maybe even teach us how to pray. Moms are a gift for us, and while some of us may have a strained relationship with our mother, or perhaps no relationship at all, we know that (in the ideal setting) the relationship between a mother and child is, in many ways, sacred.

Jesus had a mother who was specifically chosen for him, and like any mother she taught Jesus how to walk, talk, and even pray. Mary was there for the big moments of Jesus's life—including his Death and Resurrection. From the very beginning, Mary knew that she was carrying the promised Messiah—a Savior for humanity—but she didn't know the full picture. She knew Jesus was destined for great things and would save us, but how or when were beyond Mary's knowledge. Remember, Mary was human, and while she was the

27

Mother of God (a title we celebrate on this solemnity), that doesn't mean she had superhuman powers or could see the future. Mary was a normal mother with some very extraordinary experiences.

In the gospel, we read and hear that shepherds came to honor Jesus, a child they had no other connection to, and they glorified and praised God when they saw him. Can you imagine being present hours after a new child is born, and suddenly the hospital room is crowded with strange people who start singing? Many mothers (especially new mothers) would justifiably be a bit uncomfortable with the strange, foreign visitors, to say the least. Instead Mary "kept all these things, pondering them in her heart" (Lk 2:19). There is a secret to discipleship in that single line.

Mary is the Mother of God. She bears the Messiah in her womb, gives birth to him, raises him, watches his ministry, and is even present at his death. She is a witness to his Resurrection. But in all the moments leading up to that, Mary didn't know what might happen next. Instead she trusted God and reflected on the work that God was doing in each moment. We can easily get caught up in "what comes next" in our lives and miss what God is doing right now. Instead of trying to tell the future or look ahead, we could find much more peace and joy if we adopted a heart like Mary—a heart that "keeps all these things"—trusting that God knows the journey and will lead us to where we need to be.

RELATED FACT

Sheep have very poor eyesight but compensate with a strong sense of hearing. Baby sheep can identify their mother by the unique sound she makes called "bleating."

BEHIND THE SCENES

Shepherds in the time of Jesus didn't have the best reputation, despite some of the greatest biblical characters being shepherds. Ancient sources often cite them as "dishonest thieves," and they were accused of stealing members of others' flocks. Whatever history Israel had

with shepherds, the perception had changed by the first century. Shepherds weren't even allowed to fulfill a judicial office or be witnesses in a courtroom.

The appearance of shepherds may have been, for this reason, a bit unnerving to Mary and Joseph until they relayed the vision they had seen and the message they received about Jesus. St. Luke intentionally painted this picture. Whereas Matthew focused on the Magi coming from the East to worship Jesus, Luke wanted to focus on the lowly coming to give glory to God. It makes sense that those who were seen as disreputable and sinners would be some of the first to come and honor Jesus who, later on in life, would surround himself with this very kind of person.

That connection wasn't lost on St. Luke, so he made the story of the shepherds meeting Jesus a key part of the birth narrative. He wanted to remind the reader of his gospel that, from the very beginning of Jesus's life, God was calling all people to Jesus regardless of reputation, occupation, or past.

WORD PLAY

Theotokos is the Greek title for Mary, literally translated as "God-bearer" or "Mother of God." It has been used as a title for Mary since the early third century.

JOURNAL

1. The first reading includes the formula for a blessing. In what ways has God blessed you in your life?

2. Reflect on what God has done in your life. Recall any times that God intervened, answered prayers (or seemingly left prayers unanswered), and, by doing so, revealed himself to you.

3. Where do you want God to "show up" this coming year?

CHALLENGE FOR THE WEEK

Offer a prayer of thanksgiving for your mom or any other woman in your life who has acted like a mother to you. If she's still alive, spend

some quality time with her, send flowers, or call her to say thank you for all she has done in your lifetime. Thank her for the gifts she gave to you, gives to you, and will give to you throughout her constant "yes" to motherhood.

They Were Overjoyed

Epiphany of the Lord

OPENING PRAYER

Jesus, you came to save the world and destroyed death and evil for my sake. You bring joy and light to all things and seek me at all times. Help me be completely present to you. Help me let go of all things that are holding me back from you. Open my heart to your joy, peace, and redemption. Amen.

> **First Reading:** Isaiah 60:1–6
> **Responsorial Psalm:** Psalm 72:1–2, 7–8, 10–11, 12–13
> **Second Reading:** Ephesians 3:2–3a, 5–6
> **Gospel:** Matthew 2:1–12

BEYOND WORDS

Have you ever met a "big-time" celebrity? Maybe you spotted a famous actor or actress in an airport or got an autograph from a well-known athlete. Perhaps you got a selfie with a famous musician or star. If you have, you remember how excited you were. If you haven't, imagine how you'd feel if someone you really looked up to or admired all of a sudden was face-to-face with you. It'd be memorable to say the least—definitely social-media worthy.

The Magi were excited when they saw a star, too, but for very different reasons. The star they beheld was one filled with both promise and mystery. The heavenly orb led them to an even greater heavenly reality in a manger. The prophet Isaiah told us it was going to happen, but it was the Gentiles (non-Jews) who cracked this code. Their arrival and imminent worship did more than reveal the baby's royal identity; it revealed the depth and breadth of God's plan to save us. Jesus was coming for everyone, not just the "chosen" Jewish people.

Did you catch that? The wise men thought they were seeking the Lord only to realize that the God of the universe (not even "their" god") was actually the one seeking *them*! In the second reading we hear how this beautiful mystery was being made known, and we are all invited to behold this mystery, to contemplate it, and to celebrate it. If the fact that God came to save you from death does not fill you with indescribable joy, it may be time to ponder this fact on your knees before the God of the universe, just like the Magi did. Jesus is waiting in the tabernacle. Show up, bring your gifts, and follow in their oh-so-wise footsteps.

RELATED FACT

Scripture never names the Magi. In fact, the Bible doesn't even say there are three "kings," only three gifts. Tradition tells us (through St. Bede) that the names of the Magi are Gaspar, Melchior, and Balthazar. Gaspar is often depicted as a younger, beardless, and red-haired man. Melchior is usually seen as an older man with white hair and long white beard. Balthazar is normally depicted as a middle-aged man of dark complexion with a heavy beard.

BEHIND THE SCENES

It can be difficult for us to truly appreciate how challenging St. Paul's mission was within the early Church. Trained as a (Jewish) rabbi but called to be "the apostle to the Gentiles," St. Paul had the unenviable task of evangelizing the non-Jews and welcoming them into God's chosen family amid Jews who, from birth, hated them. On top of that, before St. Paul's conversion, he (Saul) was the one hunting down the new Christians and condemning them to death. It's easy to see why St. Paul had few friends who completely trusted him when his missionary work began and had enemies everywhere who felt he had lost his mind or sacrificed his soul.

This backdrop makes the second reading even more impressive. St. Paul tells the Ephesians that the Gentiles are not merely "tacked on" to God's open door to salvation but equal to God's Chosen People, the Jews, as "co-heirs, members of the same body" (Eph 3:6). St. Paul is giving the Gentiles not a lower status but one equal in stature before God and man. Given this background on the second reading, one can more easily see why the Church, in her wisdom, decided to place this epistle within the cycle of readings for Epiphany Sunday.

WORD PLAY

The word *epiphany* comes from the Latin *epiphania*, meaning "to reveal." For the first several centuries of the Church it was actually the Feast of Epiphany, even more than Christmas, that celebrated the "revelation" of the Incarnation. Epiphany Sunday is a celebration of the reality that God took flesh at an appointed time in history and that God was announcing and offering salvation to *all*, not just the Chosen People of Israel.

JOURNAL

1. The Savior of the world seeks you. How can you present yourself to him? Go to the chapel? Go to Mass? Pray more frequently?

2. Through the sacraments, specifically Baptism and Confirmation, God gives us spiritual gifts to help us build his kingdom. What gifts do you have that you can use for his glory?

3. Are you coming to Jesus with joy? If not, what is holding you back from being joyful? How can you be joyful through the midst of what is holding you back?

CHALLENGE FOR THE WEEK

The best way to encounter Jesus is to go to Mass. The Mass is the closest we can be to God on Earth. This week, pick a day to go to daily Mass. Show up where Christ is sure to be, just like the Magi showed up at the Nativity. If you cannot attend a daily Mass, go to an adoration chapel near you to pray when you are available. The first step of prayer is to actually show up.

Heirs to the Throne

Baptism of the Lord

OPENING PRAYER

Come, Holy Spirit. Heavenly Father, you have revealed to us the promise of salvation through your only Son, Jesus Christ. You have sent the Holy Spirit to be at work with you and the Son to complete the plan of our salvation. I thank you, Lord, for making me a child of God by my Baptism. Forgive me if I do not love this gift well enough. Holy Spirit, anoint me with your peace and set a fire within my heart to be an authentic disciple of Christ in this world. Amen.

> **First Reading:** Isaiah 42:1–4, 6–7
> **Responsorial Psalm:** Psalm 29:1–2, 3–4, 3, 9–10
> **Second Reading:** Acts 10:34–38
> **Gospel:** Matthew 3:13–17

BEYOND WORDS

You're doing the laundry and you find a twenty-dollar bill in your pocket. Your raffle ticket gets picked for the grand prize. Your favorite team wins the championship. Some news seems too good to be true.

You are a child of God. In God's mind, you are not just a creation or creature or slave or servant—you are his son or daughter.

Let that sink in.

That truth is a cause for celebration. That truth deserves gratitude and worship and an outpouring of love on our part, as this week's psalm suggests. God is our protector and our promise in the face of danger, hardship, and fear (as we are told in the first reading). We know this because we have a special relationship with God through his Son, Jesus. Our Baptism is a gift almost too good to be true. It literally changes our relationship with God because it literally changes us.

The fact is that God looks at us—all the baptized—in a different way and through a new lens: not as servants (first reading) but as children (gospel). You can read more about this in the Behind the Scenes section.

In getting baptized himself (though, strictly speaking, Jesus had no "need" for it), Jesus gives us an example to follow. Filled with the Holy Spirit and power, Jesus goes forth on a mission to do good (second reading), all the while glorifying his Father in his every word and deed. We are challenged, as baptized sons and daughters, to do likewise. We have no reason to fear because, as all the readings reaffirm, God is with us and no one will defeat us.

RELATED FACT

There are only three places in all the gospels where we hear God the Father speak audibly. We "hear" the first instance this week at the baptism of Jesus in the Jordan. We also hear God the Father's voice at the Transfiguration (see Matthew 17:5) and before the Last Supper and Passion of our Lord (see John 12:28).

BEHIND THE SCENES

Every Sunday, the Church picks Mass readings that complement one another thematically. Sometimes the link between them is evident, and sometimes it can be difficult to unveil and make an obvious "connection." In this week's first reading and gospel, we see a clear biblical and theological link between the prophet Isaiah and the Lord Jesus, but at the same time, the two readings also reveal a stark difference.

In Isaiah, we see God revealing and announcing Isaiah as his chosen *servant*. God places his spirit upon Isaiah, rejoices over him, protects him, and seeks to bring justice through him. Likewise, in Matthew's gospel, we see Jesus as the "new" Isaiah. The Spirit descends upon Jesus, God says he is "well pleased," and he rejoices over Jesus. He is going to "fulfill all righteousness"—a just act.

The key difference illuminated between the two episodes, however, can easily be missed when hearing the gospel proclaimed. This

difference is seen in the spoken words of God the Father, referring to Jesus not merely as a "servant" but as "my Son." The relationship is not master to servant but, rather, father to son. It's not based on performance or role but on unconditional love and familial bond.

Because we, the faithful, are baptized sons and daughters of God, we enjoy the latter identity as children. When we are baptized in Christ, we partake (take part) in his divine sonship to the Father. We get to move out of the "servant" quarters and are moved straight into the family mansion, being given every blessing that comes with it. In that, when a baptized Christian serves God, it is not out of obligation (like in the master-servant relationship) but out of a loving response.

It's because of this distinction that we are able to hear and receive this reality that many Christians still struggle to fathom. Namely, when God says he is "well pleased," he isn't just talking about Jesus but—through the grace of sacrament—he is well pleased with all of his children. Isaiah, as beloved as he was, never knew this kind of relationship, but we do. Praise God!

WORD PLAY

The psalmist speaks of God's great and "holy splendor." The word *splendor* comes from the Latin *splendere*, meaning "to shine brightly."

JOURNAL

1. Do you treat your relationship with God as master-servant or father-child? Is it intimate or rooted in fear? Why is that?

2. How different would the world be if people lived out the truth of their Baptism? How do you let the truth of your Baptism affect how you live?

3. Are you in the habit of asking the Holy Spirit to guide and transform your life? In what areas of your life do you need the Holy Spirit's intervention the most?

CHALLENGE FOR THE WEEK

Find someone this week to hold you accountable for a way you want to grow in your relationship with God. Try to meet with this person and pray together sometime this week.

ORDINARY TIME

A Light to the Nations

Second Sunday in Ordinary Time

OPENING PRAYER

Heavenly Father, help me to see myself as you see me. Open my eyes to the reasons you delight in me. I know that you have crafted specific qualities in me to accomplish a certain mission. Today, help me to realize that I am your beloved and will not fail with you by my side. Amen.

> **First Reading:** Isaiah 49:3, 5–6
> **Responsorial Psalm:** Psalm 40:2, 4, 7–8, 8–9, 10
> **Second Reading:** 1 Corinthians 1:1–3
> **Gospel:** John 1:29–34

BEYOND WORDS

Have you ever used too much soap on dishes or in the laundry and "enjoyed" the never-ending, overflowing stream of bubbles? Most modern soap is so concentrated that less than a dime's worth can clean most things. Put simply, a little can do a lot when you add water to it.

When Isaiah came onto the scene, Israel was not doing very well. The surrounding world powers often picked on tiny Israel and—due to their own trust issues and infidelity to God—God allowed his children to be bullied and enslaved as a result of their own sin, even though God loved them dearly. The first reading reminds us that God can do great things with very little. Israel will become "a light to the nations" (Is 49:6). Through the second reading, St. Paul is reminding the new Church in Corinth that although they may be small in number and in power, they are holy and mighty in Christ. While St. John the Baptist lived as more of a hermit with questionable fashion sense and dietary habits, God used this "small" and seemingly

insignificant desert dweller to put the Pharisees in their place, the people on notice, and the Lord upon his mission.

You might look in the mirror and see everything you are "lacking." You might wonder what you really have to offer the world. God doesn't see you that way. He doesn't focus on what you seem to lack but on how you love. He sees all he designed you to be and all that you can become by the help of his grace. You are greater than you can imagine. You can become a saint—a true light to the nations—and all God needs is your "yes." What do you say?

RELATED FACT

We often hear the names "Jacob" and "Israel" in scripture, but do we understand anything about them? Jacob is Isaac's (younger) son and Abraham's grandson. Israel is known to many people as a place in the Middle East but to far fewer as a person. After a night of literally wrestling with God at Peniel (see Genesis 32), God changed Jacob's name to *Israel*, which means "one who contends/strives with God." So, the nation of Israel has its history in the twelve tribes of Israel—tribes that began with Jacob's twelve sons.

BEHIND THE SCENES

"Lamb of God" is one of the most common titles associated with Christ. It is the first title uttered by St. John the Baptist as our Lord approached the Jordan River in this week's gospel. While people today may be confused as to how a lamb can take away sins, it made perfect sense to the people the Baptist was addressing. Christ's title as the "Lamb of God" points us not only to his mission, but also to his identity.

While it is far too deep to do justice to in this brief section, it will suffice to say that sacrifice was (and still is) a vital element within worship. Sacrifice is one of our most basic human actions and needs. In sacrificing something to God, we remember who he is and who we are not; we demonstrate that God is greater than we are and that all good gifts come from him.

41

During the tenth plague in Exodus, God prescribed a way for his people to be protected from death. He ordered every household to select a lamb, slaughter it, eat its flesh, and cover the wooden door-post of their home with the lamb's blood (see Exodus 12) in order to avoid the death of the firstborn male child (both human and animal; see Exodus 12:29).

Animal sacrifice was quite commonplace in the ancient world, so God was using a well-known practice but reorienting it to him (rather than to false gods). In fact, the animals God commanded the Hebrews to sacrifice were actually gods to other people, further making God's point regarding his status as the one, true God. In commanding his people to spill these animals' blood and then eat them, God made the gravest sin for the Egyptians (in this case) the path to forgiveness for his children (the Israelites). God had taken the Israelites out of Egypt, but in calling for this bloody sacrifice, God was trying to "take Egypt out of the Israelites."

WORD PLAY

The word *Pharisee* comes from a Hebrew word that means "separate." Pharisees separated themselves from most of society, which they considered sinful, in an effort to stay clean. At the time of Jesus, they were the popular religious political party. What's vital to understand about the Pharisees is that they were very legalistic and followed the Law of Moses in extremely exacting ways (see Matthew 9:14; 23:15; Luke 18:12). While their intentions seemed pure and their creed was solid, their religion was more about form and function than surrender or humility; they obeyed the letter of the law but ignored the spirit of it. They were very self-righteous (see Matthew 9; Luke 18) and, as a result, Jesus had some strong words for them (see Matthew 12:9; 16:1–4).

JOURNAL

1. Think of a specific talent you have. Why did God give you this talent? How have you used it in the past? How could you use it better in the future?

2. When was a time that God did more or blessed you more than you were expecting? What does this tell you about God?

3. Do you struggle to recognize your talents? Why? How can you overcome this?

4. Other people in your life are beautiful and wonderful and talented, too. Who is someone in your life who could use a reminder that they are wonderfully made? How could you help them realize this?

CHALLENGE FOR THE WEEK

Is there a quality you have that isn't from the Lord? For example, if you've noticed you're really struggling with impatience, ask God confidently to rid you of that throughout this week.

I Belong to Christ
Third Sunday in Ordinary Time

OPENING PRAYER

Heavenly Father, you have claimed me as your own. Not only this, but you have given me the Church—made up of brothers and sisters, all claimed by you. Help me to see my identity as this, your child, and nothing else. My worth is in you, who is love, joy, and peace. Amen.

> **First Reading:** Isaiah 8:23–9:3
> **Responsorial Psalm:** Psalm 27:1, 4, 13–14
> **Second Reading:** 1 Corinthians 1:10–13, 17
> **Gospel:** Matthew 4:12–23

BEYOND WORDS

Where do you draw your worth? Is it from how many friends or followers you have in your online profile or how many likes you receive on your posts? Is it your title or accomplishments at work or your home or your kids' accomplishments? What external things offer you attention or esteem or validation?

Is that where God wants you to look for your worth or to seek your identity? You may feel forgotten, like those in the regions of Zebulun and Naphtali (first reading), or divided like the people in Corinth (second reading). You might draw your worth from your job or family name (gospel), but the Lord wants your whole heart, regardless of your situation. Even if you feel like he isn't there, make no mistake! God is pursuing you and inviting you even more deeply into his life, just like he did for the apostles beside Galilee that day.

He wants to be the sole source of your worth and your joy. He invites you to come and be like him. He wants to hear you joyfully utter—no matter what you are feeling—that "I belong to Christ." If you can say that with total sincerity, people will follow you straight back to him.

RELATED FACT

Zebulun and Naphtali are not just the names of regions but the names of two of the original Israelite tribes (and sons of Jacob). These two regions were the first to be destroyed by the Assyrians around 730 BC. Jesus traveled there to begin the symbolic work of restoring Israel, starting with the earliest victims from among the twelve original tribes.

BEHIND THE SCENES

St. Paul arrived in Corinth as part of his second missionary journey, most likely sometime between AD 50 and AD 53. He helped start the Church in Corinth by living among the Corinthians for eighteen months (see Acts 18:11), but he was unable to remain in the city and oversee its spiritual growth (see Acts 18:12–18). Unfortunately, a lot of scandalous behavior began to emerge within the Church in Corinth after the apostle left.

Through word of mouth, St. Paul heard about some of the gross sins the Christians had been committing, and in the First Letter to the Corinthians he was writing to encourage them to reject their immoral behavior and to renew their commitment to a life grounded in the love of Christ (see 1 Corinthians 10:6–13). Additionally, as we see in this week's passage, he urges them to live in solidarity, communion, and fellowship and to bring unity rather than division.

WORD PLAY

Who is this *Cephas* that we hear about in Paul's Epistle to the Corinthians? Cephas is Peter. Most Catholics know that Jesus changed Simon's name to Peter, which means "the Rock" (see Matthew 16:18). Peter or *Petros* is the masculine form of the Greek term *petra*, which means "rock." What some don't know, however, is that Jesus spoke Aramaic in everyday life, and the Aramaic for Peter is *Kepha* or *Cephas*, depending on who is translating it. St. John explains it to us in his own gospel with the statement: "He brought him to Jesus. Jesus looked at him, and said, 'So you are Simon the son of John? You shall be called Cephas' (which means Peter)" (John 1:42).

JOURNAL

1. From where do you draw your worth and identity beyond God? Professional achievements? Financial success? Be honest with yourself. Where do you find affirmation/validation beyond God?

2. Why is it so easy to put your worth into something that is not God?

3. When we put our worth in God, we become invested in the Church, which is a family. How can you help your brothers and sisters put their worth in Christ?

CHALLENGE FOR THE WEEK

Every day this week, do something good for someone else. Maybe you serve at a soup kitchen, offer to watch someone's kids, give up time in your day to help a friend, or say a Rosary for a specific person. Get creative and offer up a part of yourself, big or small, every day. By serving others, you are uniting yourself with the Church and with God.

Your Reward Will Be Great in Heaven

Fourth Sunday in Ordinary Time

OPENING PRAYER

God, I am not perfect. I make mistakes. Sometimes, I believe I am more powerful than I really am. Sometimes, I take things into my own hands and I do not trust in you. Yet you love me anyway. Open my eyes to see you more directly, my ears to hear you more clearly, and my heart to love you. Help me to trust in you and to be your humble servant. Amen.

First Reading: Zephaniah 2:3; 3:12–13
Responsorial Psalm: Psalm 146:6–7, 8–9, 9–10
Second Reading: 1 Corinthians 1:26–31
Gospel: Matthew 5:1–12a

BEYOND WORDS

If given the option, would you rather be a king or a peasant, a queen or a servant? Would you rather be the star on the stage or the janitor cleaning the stadium after the concert? If given the option, would you want to be the star athlete on the field or the guy selling peanuts in the stands?

Very few people would choose the latter and opt for the "low end" of the flowchart of power. As the prophet Zephaniah reminds us in the first reading, we must seek humility, for in doing so, we honor and find the Lord. St. Paul, too, warns the people in Corinth (in the second reading) of the dangers of thinking ourselves too wise in our own estimation. God chooses "the foolish"; he tells them (and us) "to shame the wise" (1 Cor 1:27). To think we know all is pure pride and to admit we do not is the root of humility.

When our Lord offers these famous Beatitudes during the Sermon on the Mount, we gain invaluable insight into the mind and

heart of God: Those who appear to have nothing actually have it all. The souls who are humble and small and "forgotten" are the ones who (will) actually "get it" (heaven). It's natural in our humanity to desire the power, but it's freeing to finally realize that our power is rooted in our humility and in Christ alone.

RELATED FACT

Each one of the Beatitudes is 140 characters or less. Jesus is the master of profound depth with extraordinary simplicity.

BEHIND THE SCENES

Jesus's famous Sermon on the Mount (from which these Beatitudes are taken) is said to have taken place on a mountain in St. Matthew's gospel. In St. Luke's gospel, however, the sermon is said to have taken place "on the plain." Some people over the years have pointed to this discrepancy as a "proof" that the gospels are unreliable historical narratives. On the contrary, small discrepancies actually point to separate sources and, thus, make the circulating gospel narratives even more reliable. Whether or not the sermon took place on a mountain or on a plain matters little to the truths Jesus shared. The difference can be easily explained, too. The word *plain* actually translates to "level place" in the Greek. It's entirely possible that St. Luke was referring to a level place (like a small plateau) upon the side of a mountain. It's plausible, too, that Jesus delivered the sermon several times over his three-year ministry and that Luke's version was a separate or second occurrence of Jesus blowing people's minds with the Beatitudes and the sermon on heaven, hell, and salvation that followed.

WORD PLAY

St. Matthew begins these eight Beatitudes with the word *blessed*. From the Greek *makarios*, *blessed* doesn't mean you're just "on God's good side" or that you are theologically "lucky" but, rather, that you are righteous before God. The blessed souls are the ones who know

48

God, whose sins are forgiven, and who love and follow him no matter the circumstance, for theirs is the kingdom of heaven.

JOURNAL

1. Reflecting on the first few questions given in the Beyond Words section, how does choosing the lesser bring us closer to Christ?

2. Have you ever chosen the lesser? If so, how did it strengthen you? If not, what opportunities do you have to choose the lesser?

3. Do you trust in God's will, or do you take matters in your own hands? How can you better submit to God's wisdom?

4. How is God calling you to give up your power?

CHALLENGE FOR THE WEEK

Write each of the Beatitudes down on a note card. Every morning, for the next eight days, pick one to reflect on and try to live out that beatitude during the day. As a bonus, keep a journal of your reflections and prayer with each beatitude through the week.

God's Response
Presentation of the Lord

OPENING PRAYER

God, your ways are bigger than my ways. And thank goodness for that. You see the entire picture while I see but a small glimpse. Help me to have confidence in you and your plan for my life. Help me to have peace that while I am reactive, you are proactive. Be with me as I enter into your Word today. Amen.

> **First Reading:** Malachi 3:1–4
> **Responsorial Psalm:** Psalm 24:7, 8, 9, 10
> **Second Reading:** Hebrews 2:14–18
> **Gospel:** Luke 2:22–40

BEYOND WORDS

God is not reactive.

Sometimes—actually, *most of the time*—we make the small-minded, short-sighted mistake of thinking that God is like us. While we are made in his "image and likeness" (Gn 1:26), that does not mean that God is like us in our thinking, reactiveness, or humanity. God is divine. He is perfect, sinless, and never, ever "reactive." Even in moments when God's righteous anger flares up in the Old Testament or in the gospel with the money changers or Pharisees, it is not a reaction as much as it is a "response."

God sends messages, warnings, and prophecies. God normally foretells and foreshadows what he is going to do long before he ever does it. In this week's readings, we see this played out, yet again. God speaks through the prophet Malachi (first reading) of a coming "messenger" who will "prepare the way before me." Here, God is pointing toward St. John the Baptist, which might not seem that spectacular, until we realize that Malachi was prophesying about John the Baptist *well over four hundred years before John the Baptist was even born*! Does

that sound like God didn't have a plan, or was "reacting" to what was going on in the world when he formed the Baptist in Elizabeth's womb?

That's how Simeon and Anna (in this week's gospel) knew that the baby being presented before them was the promised Messiah. The pair *knew the prophecies and traditions* of old that were written and spoken about. They knew what and who to be on the lookout for. At the same time, they were also in prayerful contemplation and communication with God. They were dialed into the Holy Spirit in a far deeper way than most of their contemporaries at the time were.

The writer to the Hebrews, too, is trying to point out God's "plan" and strategy in the second reading, a plan that unfolded and was revealed over time. Walking us all the way back to Abraham's descendants and pointing even further back to the effects of sin stemming from Eden, the author of Hebrews shows us that God was actually *proactive* in creating a way to restore the relationship humanity broke with him, by sending us the solution to sin, in Christ's Cross and Resurrection.

We are reactive, which often results in sin. God is proactive, which offers us inconceivable grace.

RELATED FACT

St. Luke makes it a point to tell us this scene happens when "the time came *for their purification* according to the law of Moses" (Lk 2:22). One might wonder why the Holy Family would have to go through a ritual of purification. Well, the Law of Moses prescribed that after birth an Israelite woman was ritually "unclean" for forty days until she offered sacrifice in the Temple in Jerusalem. This was a legalistic ritual placed on all women and couples. Much like Jesus had no need for baptism in the Jordan but put himself "under" the Law, here we see Mary, likewise, submitting to the cultural laws of her time and culture.

BEHIND THE SCENES

As St. Augustine is credited with saying (and the *Catechism* reaffirms), "The New Testament lies hidden in the Old and the Old

51

Testament is unveiled in the New" (*CCC* 129). There are countless places in the writings and books of the Old Testament where we see characters who "prefigure" or foreshadow Jesus in various ways. We see this very directly in the life of the great prophet Samuel.

There are too many parallels to list here, but in terms of this week's gospel passage, we see a beautiful example of prefigurement played out where Jesus's presentation in the Temple by Mary and Joseph echoes the dedication of Samuel in the Temple by his parents, Hannah and Elkanah. Samuel was offered to God for priestly service, too. While St. Luke does not explicitly say this of Mary and Joseph's son, the similarities in the scene do seem to imply it about Jesus.

Like Samuel, Jesus will grow in popularity, respect, and acceptance as not only a prophet, but a priest. Eventually, though, Samuel's message proved too difficult for people in power to bear, and he was rejected—just like our Lord Jesus.

WORD PLAY

The name *Simeon* in Hebrew means "one who listens intently." It's a pretty appropriate name for the one who was so dialed in to the Holy Spirit's voice and messages, huh?

JOURNAL

1. Why is it difficult to let go of things we own?

2. What parts of your life are you afraid to offer back to God? Why?

3. Do you believe that God has a plan for your life and that his plan is good? Why?

4. What can you do to trust God more with your life?

CHALLENGE FOR THE WEEK

Every day this week, pray this simple prayer to start each morning: "Jesus, I desire your will. Please help me to see your hand in even my smallest moments. Amen."

Be Healed

Fifth Sunday in Ordinary Time

OPENING PRAYER

Jesus, Divine Physician, you heal every wound and vanish every scar. You make the blind see and the deaf hear. Open my eyes to see you more clearly. Open my ears to hear you more easily. Give me the grace to serve you joyfully and draw me closer to you. Amen.

First Reading: Isaiah 58:7–10
Responsorial Psalm: Psalm 112:4–5, 6–7, 8–9
Second Reading: 1 Corinthians 2:1–5
Gospel: Matthew 5:13–16

BEYOND WORDS

If you've ever witnessed an accident or found yourself in a situation where someone needed emergency medical attention, then you know how stressful it can be. As people wait for an ambulance to arrive, other people desperately begin searching for a doctor or nurse or anyone with medical or emergency training. If viewed through this lens of urgency, action, and wisdom, this week's readings have a similar theme.

As Christians, we are called to act, to serve, and to help the Lord in his work of salvation here on Earth. To extend the analogy, if Christ is the divine surgeon in the emergency room of the sanctuary and confessional, we who know him and follow him are like his paramedics. We help bring the sick to the physician. We aren't supposed to hide our light but to shine brightly, as the gospel challenges us. God's children must be prepared to act and to serve in tangible ways, ways that will save lives (and souls), as we see in Isaiah's admonition. If we are humble enough to trust in God's wisdom and power—the first-aid training we have received—we will be prepared to share his knowledge and his truth with the souls dying for it, spiritually.

53

If we see the culture for where it really is—a culture of darkness and increasing hopelessness—there will be a sense of urgency for us to respond. Souls are perishing, and the modern Christian must be prepared to become small (in humility) but not act small (with false humility or timidity). God wants us to act and to do so in a way that unleashes his power and brings him all the glory.

RELATED FACT

Salt was a very valuable commodity in Jesus's time. It was used as a preservative for food (since there weren't any refrigerators). It was of such great value to people that Roman taxes were sometimes paid with salt rather than coins. The phrase "he's not worth his salt" came from this practice.

BEHIND THE SCENES

How can a lamp, placed on a lampstand, light an entire house? If you were to go home tonight and only turn on a lamp in your living room, would it light up your bedroom? This analogy that our Lord uses is usually lost on modern readers, but it teaches us a great deal about Israelite culture two thousand years ago. In Jesus's day, the lamp would illuminate the entire house because many of the houses were only one large room. While some houses were larger, a majority of the homes were one bigger-sized interior space along with an outer courtyard where cooking and gathering occurred. In the lines that follow, we will hear the Lord tell us to "go into your room and shut the door" (Mt 6:6). Knowing that most houses had no separate "bedroom," the listeners of the day would have naturally inferred from the Lord's context that their inner room was not an architectural space but, rather, their own heart.

WORD PLAY

In this Gospel passage on salt and light, Jesus is teaching His *disciples*. The word *disciple* comes from the Latin *discipulus*, meaning "learner." Simply put, a disciple is one who sits at the feet of and learns from the master. Learning was active in Christ's day; it was and is not only theoretical, but also practical. For the disciples to actually be the salt and the light, they needed not only to "hear" what the Lord was saying, but also to live it out in their daily lives.

JOURNAL

1. Before we can bring others to health, we must be healthy ourselves. Is there anything from your past that has created a wound? Has it been healed? If not, how can you open yourself up to God's healing power?

2. Have you ever brought someone to Christ who needed healing? How did that experience change you?

3. How is God calling you to bring others to him (or bring him to others)? Is there a kind of service that you feel a pull toward?

CHALLENGE FOR THE WEEK

One way that we can serve others and bring them closer to Christ is to be hospitable. Meeting someone's needs by sacrificing yourself, belongings, or time is what Jesus showed us to do while walking on this Earth. This week, be hospitable. Open your home to visitors for dinner. Do a random act of kindness. Go out of your way for someone who's not expecting it. Service and sacrifice for others always glorifies God.

The Wonders of His Law
Sixth Sunday in Ordinary Time

OPENING PRAYER

Heavenly Father, you see that I desire freedom and, in your generosity, have given me a guide to live as freely as possible. Give me the grace to follow the Ten Commandments so I can achieve greater union with you. As I reflect on your laws today, I renounce my sinful ways and commit to following you even more closely than before. Amen.

> **First Reading:** Sirach 15:15–20
> **Responsorial Psalm:** Psalm 119:1–5, 17–18, 33–34
> **Second Reading:** 1 Corinthians 2:6–10
> **Gospel:** Matthew 5:17–37

BEYOND WORDS

Do rules exist to ruin your life or to save it? Consider the warnings on a medicine bottle, a speed-limit sign, or the signal at a crosswalk. Are these examples of things designed to control or preserve your life?

The Commandments are often seen more as rules than opportunities, a list of "thou shalt nots" designed to limit our fun rather than invitations to grow in love and virtue. The first reading from Sirach should be shared with every modern mind as it clearly and succinctly points out that the Commandments are all about our choices. Do we opt for self or for God? We see the relationship beyond mere rules. This same theme is furthered by Christ in St. Matthew's gospel as we hear God implore us to live not for ourselves but for others and for him. Why does all this matter? God desires an eternal relationship with us, one free of sin and death, shame and guilt. God wants us to live with him forever and, as St. Paul explains it to the Corinthians in the second reading (echoing Isaiah), what God has prepared for us we cannot even fathom.

Oh, if only we meant the words of the psalm and really prayed that our eyes would be opened. If only we found God's law wonder-filled and awesome and his love proactive.

We have to ask ourselves if we seek the Lord or the loophole when it comes to the Commandments, because sin is not as much about breaking a set of rules as it is about breaking the Father's heart.

RELATED FACT

Gehenna, we are told by Jesus, is a fiery place you do *not* want to visit. Used as an analogy for hell, Gehenna was an awful place. Over the years some have claimed that Gehenna was a "garbage dump" outside of Jerusalem's southern side, in the Valley of Hinnom, where refuse and even corpses were burned. The truth, however, is that there is no biblical evidence to support the theory of the burning trash dump. Archeology, too, has given us very little support of this theory. The Old Testament pointed to the location as evil because of pagan cult practices that occurred there, including human sacrifices. The prophet Jeremiah even cursed the location. Isaiah wrote about it, too, mentioning fire and how those who rebel against the Lord would die there. It was most likely from this prophetic tradition that Jesus was pulling his analogy and not from an actual spot of waste disposal.

BEHIND THE SCENES

Sometimes people mistakenly reduce the Sermon on the Mount to just the "feel-good" Beatitudes. In truth, St. Matthew's version of the sermon is more than 2,400 words, of which the Beatitudes make up less than 200. The fact of the matter is that probably nowhere else in the gospels is Jesus more emphatic about the realities of heaven and hell and the reality of objective truth than he is between Matthew chapters 5 and 7. Flipping through these 2,000 words, you'll see our Lord discuss following the Law, dealing with anger, the severity of adultery, the reality of divorce, the truth about hell, and warnings against swearing false oaths and retaliating against our enemies. Jesus discusses not only the need for prayer, fasting, and almsgiving, but also the dangers of earthly treasures, worldliness, being judgmental, profane living, false prophets, and self-righteousness. The Sermon on the Mount provides both a foundation for the Church's moral teaching and an invitation to sanctity for all who profess Jesus Christ as Lord.

WORD PLAY

You may have noticed the random word *raqa* used in this week's gospel passage. *Raqa* is an Aramaic translation of *reka*, which was used by Jews to denote contempt for another. As a way of showing their disdain for another, they would invoke the term *raqa*, which actually came from a Hebrew word meaning "to spit."

JOURNAL

1. Can you think of a time when you didn't follow the rules or a guide? What did you learn from the experience?

2. What is a specific commandment you really struggle with? How has it damaged your relationships with others? What can you do to overcome it?

3. An important part of your relationship with Christ is receiving God's mercy. When you fall away from the Lord, do you truly believe that God has forgiven you and is thankful for your return?

CHALLENGE FOR THE WEEK

This week, try being obedient to every law in your life. Follow the laws of the Lord and of the land (don't speed or text while driving, for instance). Reflect on your experience at the end of the week. You can do this!

Love Your Enemies

Seventh Sunday in Ordinary Time

OPENING PRAYER

God, you are love. Everything you are contains an unfathomable amount of love. You are love in its purest way. You are selfless and humble. I, as your child, am called to love as you love—not only my friends, but my enemies. Lord, give me the grace to love those who are hard to love. Help others see you in me as I love them like you. Amen.

> **First Reading:** Leviticus 19:1–2, 17–18
> **Responsorial Psalm:** Psalm 103:1–2, 3–4, 8, 10, 12–13
> **Second Reading:** 1 Corinthians 3:16–23
> **Gospel:** Matthew 5:38–48

BEYOND WORDS

In this week's gospel we hear Jesus speaking as simply and plainly as he possibly can. It's as though he's saying, "Look, it's not impressive to love people who are nice to you and whom you like back. I mean, even an atheist can do that. No, what sets you apart is how you love those people who can't stand you or whom you cannot stand."

Think about that.

That's the measure of your love: how well you love the person who is rude to you online or in line. How kind you are to the person who rolls their eyes at you, who gets frustrated with you, or who flips you off in traffic. The law put forth in Leviticus (first reading) not only warns the people against the dangers of hatred but even stipulates for them never to hold a grudge.

Think about that.

The psalm reminds us how God pardons us. Would you like the Lord to only offer you the same amount of mercy you offer to others? Psalm 103 takes the whole "forgive us our trespasses as we forgive

ORDINARY TIME

59

those who trespass against us" to an even deeper level. Forgiveness is not a one-time thing; it's a daily thing.

Think about that.

If you belong to Christ and you are a walking tabernacle (second reading), you need to consider who you are in light of Whose you are. Holiness is simple, but not easy. Step one: don't think too highly of yourself. Loving God, first, helps with that. Step two: don't think too little of others. Loving your enemies helps with that.

RELATED FACT

Jesus tells his followers that if someone "presses you into service for one mile, go two miles." At that time Palestine was under Roman occupation and rule. By law, a Roman soldier could force anyone to have to carry his equipment (if he wanted a break or needed a rest) for up to one mile. Jews could be pressed into service against their will. Here, Jesus is telling them not only not to resist but, if pressed, to offer to go "the extra mile" for the other—even for an enemy.

BEHIND THE SCENES

In this week's gospel passage, Jesus is giving new context to old laws. Borrowing heavily from the Old Testament, Jesus is calling his followers to get above and beyond what they were accustomed to doing. "An eye for an eye" was seen as legal retribution in the time of Moses. Jews were allowed to ask for and seek restitution from someone who had wronged them. Jesus, instead, challenges people to forgive wrongdoing.

Likewise, when you've been struck on your right cheek and you offer your left, the person striking you would be forced to use the back of their right hand. The Mishnah (the written-out version of the Jewish oral law/traditions), however, explained that a backhanded slap was far more egregious and insulting a practice and the victim was entitled to twice the compensation. Jesus encourages his followers to seek neither the normal nor the inflated restitution.

The tunic example also demonstrates the willingness to forego legal rights by refusing to make a claim against someone else and, instead, offering them even more. This is not God encouraging us to be victimized or abused but, instead, he asks us to look toward the care for others more than ourselves.

WORD PLAY

Perfect? How can Jesus expect us to be "perfect"? When Jesus says, "Be perfect just as your heavenly Father is perfect," he is not saying he expects us never to sin or fall in our humanity. The Lord is calling us to imitate God the Father in how we love. Jesus is challenging us to become more loving, more merciful, and more others-centered just as God is, always has been, and forever will be.

JOURNAL

1. Think about a person in your life who is really hard to love. How is God calling you to love that person? Is it by engaging them in conversation? Is it by forgiving them for something they did in the past? Is it by praying a special intention for them every day?

2. In Isaiah, God calls us not to just give what is needed but to go above and beyond what is asked of us. How can you go above and beyond in service?

3. In the last line of Matthew, we hear, "Be perfect, as your heavenly Father is perfect." What does it mean to be perfect, not in a worldly sense, but a spiritual sense? How is God calling you to perfection?

CHALLENGE FOR THE WEEK

It takes a lot of self-discipline in order to love those who are hard to love. If we let ourselves and our emotions go, we can lose what we are aiming for, which is love. In the spirit of Lent right around the corner, work on self-discipline by fasting from something. It can be sweets, caffeine, alcohol, social media; you name it. It must be something that will take work, though. You've got this.

LENT

Him Alone Shall You Serve

First Sunday of Lent

OPENING PRAYER

Jesus, you were tempted in the desert by the same one who tempted Eve in the garden. Yet you came out on top. In preparation for your Death and Resurrection, help me resist temptation to sin and failure to fast. Give me the strength to offer all temptation to you. Prepare me for this most divine victory! Amen.

> **First Reading:** Genesis 2:7–9; 3:1–7
> **Responsorial Psalm:** Psalm 51:3–4, 5–6, 12–13, 17
> **Second Reading:** Romans 5:12–19
> **Gospel:** Matthew 4:1–11

BEYOND WORDS

Can you trust God?

It's the question that has been plaguing man literally since the beginning, which we read about in today's first reading from Genesis. Notice how the serpent does not deny the existence of God, for he knew that Adam and Eve personally encountered him and that would be of no avail. No, the serpent's strategy was far more cunning: plant the seed of doubt, and encourage them to look "past" God and back to themselves. Self-focus and pride are the root of all sin. We see the devil employ the same strategy with Christ (the new Adam that we hear about in the second reading) in this gospel passage from St. Matthew.

Once Jesus is in the desert and physically depleted from fasting, the devil enters. Note how the devil attacks our Lord when he is physically compromised. Temptation often comes to us when our bodies are at odds with our souls. Pay attention to how the evil one attempts to turn Christ's attention from the Father to himself. He plays on Jesus's obvious hunger, God's fidelity (or lack thereof), and the human desire for earthly power. These are the tactics he employed then with our Lord and that he and his demons employ, still today, with us.

Lent is a purposeful journey into the desert through which our mother, the Church, seeks to help us get back to (or remain in) right order with God. Lent is a time to tackle our sin, confront our temptations, and subdue our human desires in light of our heavenly pursuit. Lent is when we don't just say we trust God but when we put our fasting where our mouth is.

RELATED FACT

Genesis tells us that "God formed the man out of the dust of the ground" (Gn 2:7). Not only is this biblical proof that God is the potter and we are the Play-Doh, but it's also where the first man gets his name. *Adam* literally comes from the Hebrew *adama*, which means "the earth."

BEHIND THE SCENES

Forty is an important number, biblically speaking. It can represent a time of blessing, a time of testing, and even a time of "probation" for disobedience, mistrust, or wrongdoing. Looking back to the beginning, however, we begin to see a pattern of forty days or forty years throughout the biblical narrative. Consider these examples:

- Forty days of rain during the great flood (see Genesis 7:17)
- Forty days of fasting by Moses (see Exodus 24:18, 34:28) and Elijah (see 1 Kings 19:8)
- Forty days of surveillance by the spies before the Promised Land (see Numbers 13:25)
- Forty days of probation for the Ninevites (see Jonah 3:4)
- Forty days of fasting (and testing) for Jesus (see Matthew 4:2)
- Forty days of Resurrection appearances before the Ascension (see Acts 1:3)

- Forty years of desert wandering for the Israelites (see Numbers 14:34)
- Forty years of peace in Israel (see Judges 3:11, 8:28)
- Forty years for Egypt to be desolated then restored (see Ezekiel 29:11, 13)

Jesus is "reliving" the history of Israel but doing so in the most faithful way. Christ's example points to the future by giving new context to the past. We participate in this death and new life in a similar way during Lent, which lasts how long? You get the idea.

WORD PLAY

Sometimes when we hear the term *serpent* in this famous passage from Genesis, we fall into the trap of envisioning a rattlesnake curled up in a tree (as has often been the depiction in artwork and at Vacation Bible School). The Hebrew people had a much different image. The Hebrew word used for "serpent" is *nahash*, which in apocalyptic and poetic stories did not denote a small snake but, rather, a large, menacing, dragon-like sea creature. We see this type of creature represented elsewhere in the Bible as being an enemy of the Lord and his people (see Job 26:13; Isaiah 27:1; Amos 9:3).

JOURNAL

1. What does it mean to trust in God?

2. We hear the phrase "trust in God" a lot, but do we actually do it? Do you truly trust in God, his wisdom, and his plan for you? How is he calling you to trust in him?

3. Our fasting during Lent is a way to help us resist the temptation of sin throughout the rest of the year by conditioning our will. Is there a sin that you struggle with that this time of Lent can help you conquer?

4. In order to resist temptation, we must stay away from anything that is tempting. What do you have to stay away from in order to keep your Lenten promise?

CHALLENGE FOR THE WEEK

During Lent, it is good to fast from something to unite yourself more closely with God. However, on top of fasting, you can also add something into your life that you do not normally do. This can be praying a Rosary every day, making your bed every morning, and so on. This week, add a daily activity that takes discipline to accomplish.

Go Forth

Second Sunday of Lent

OPENING PRAYER

God, I thank you for the abundant blessings you've given me. I pray that I will never forget your goodness, no matter what trials may come my way. I thank you for the gift of hope and ask for the strength to endure any and all suffering. Help me to be faithful to you, my Lord, for you are always faithful to me. Amen.

> **First Reading:** Genesis 12:1–4a
> **Responsorial Psalm:** Psalm 33:4–5, 18–19, 20, 22
> **Second Reading:** 2 Timothy 1:8b–10
> **Gospel:** Matthew 17:1–9

BEYOND WORDS

There is a challenge that exists in the Christian life: How are you present to the day while keeping your eyes and hearts set on the future? In other words, how do we hope in heaven and put our trust in what is to come when we are enduring hardships and struggles in the present day? St. Paul outlines this challenge in the second reading and, in his letter, inspires St. Timothy to lean into the grace of God and put up with hardships, trusting that it is worth it in the end.

It is difficult to trust fully in God when life isn't turning out as you had hoped. Just look to Abraham in the first reading. God is asking him to move his entire tribe to a new land, away from his comfort zone and normal life. It is only after Abram demonstrates his full trust in God *that day* that he will be ready for future blessings.

This famous gospel scene of the Transfiguration is God giving his closest three disciples a glimpse into their future glory. It was so glorious that they didn't want to leave. And all that awaited them at the base of that mountain was more hardship, uncertainty, and eventual suffering. It's with this challenge in mind—present struggle

for future reward—that we embrace this season of Lent, a season that urges us to keep our perspective because pain is temporary but victory is eternal.

RELATED FACT

While the Bible does not explicitly say the location where the Transfiguration took place, tradition holds that it happened upon Mount Tabor, which is located roughly five miles east of Nazareth in lower Galilee.

BEHIND THE SCENES

One of the Luminous Mysteries and most famous gospel scenes, the Transfiguration is a story with a whole lot of levels of meaning and where the Old and New Testaments converge in amazing ways. Jesus's face shining forth "like the sun" actually points back to when Moses's face was shining so brightly as he descended another mountain, Sinai, in Exodus chapter 34. Moses's face, however, merely *reflected* God's glory, while Jesus is the source of the radiant glory atop Mount Tabor. Jesus's white "as light" clothing points to the "Ancient One" described in the book of Daniel as well as to the angel at the tomb later in Matthew.

The similarities between Moses and Elijah and Jesus are noteworthy, too. All three fasted for forty days, encountered God atop mountains, and represented "the voice of God" to the Jewish people. When we see the shadow cast over them, we are reminded of the cloud in the wilderness that "overshadowed" Moses's tent of meeting in Exodus. The "tents" mentioned here by Peter would have been like the tents constructed and dwelt in during the Jewish Feast of Tabernacles. Yes, the word for "tent" is *tabernacle*. In the end, both Moses and Elijah "prefigured" and set the stage for Christ. Seeing these two figures who represent the old covenant's "law and prophets" present at the Transfiguration alongside Jesus demonstrates that the entire Old Testament points to Jesus as the fulfillment of the promise and

the long-awaited Messiah (whose identity was just confirmed in the preceding episode in Matthew chapter 16).

WORD PLAY

The name *Abram* is Hebrew and loosely means "father of many." The deep irony is that at this point in the story, Abram (and his wife Sarai) are still childless. Though they had no kids of their own and were advanced in age, the name demonstrated the timelessness of God's perfect plan. Later in Genesis, God changes Abram's name to *Abraham*, which means "father of a great many" because through his son Isaac and grandson Jacob (Israel), the tribe and nation would grow exponentially.

JOURNAL

1. Why do you think God asks us to endure suffering? Do you think he leaves you to face it alone?

2. Do you know someone who is suffering, who could use your prayers or support?

3. Peter suggests setting up camp on the mountaintop, but Jesus still has work for them to do down in the valley. How is God using you "down in the valley"? Where are you serving in his name, and why do you do it?

4. How has God blessed you recently?

CHALLENGE FOR THE WEEK

Fast from hot showers, sweets, or a luxury you value, and offer that fasting for others who are suffering. Pick someone specific, such as a friend, a challenging soul at work, impoverished people in a third-world country, people affected by a specific disaster, people in prison, or the hospitalized. Doing so will encourage you to continue to fast even when you are tempted to indulge.

What Are You Waiting For?

Third Sunday of Lent

OPENING PRAYER

God, you search me and you know me. You know my deepest wounds, secrets, and desires. You call me into you, into love. You take into account all of my desires, and you know what will bring me the most joy. Help me accept your love with an open heart. I trust in you. Amen.

> **First Reading:** Exodus 17:3–7
> **Responsorial Psalm:** Psalm 95:1–2, 6–7, 8–9
> **Second Reading:** Romans 5:1–2, 5–8
> **Gospel:** John 4:5–42

BEYOND WORDS

Are you following God with all of your heart? Have you surrendered your entire life to him? If so, what was it that finally caused you to abandon your will for his? If not, why not? What are you waiting for? What *more* would God need to do for you to finally follow him with everything you have and are?

These are not new questions. These are the same questions people have needed to answer and face for thousands of years. The Israelites wandering in the desert with Moses were freed from centuries of slavery and captivity by miraculous works of God, only to later doubt his providence and his love as they thirsted in the desert. When the Samaritan woman of the gospel interacts with Jesus, he points out how she has satiated her thirst for love in fleeting relationships. Jesus's thirst was not for water that day but for her salvation and her ultimate happiness. Just as Jesus drew near to the woman at the well and just as God drew near to his people through Moses, Christ is still drawing near to us and desiring to save us. He didn't wait for us to get it together. No, we are reminded in the second reading that "while we were yet sinners Christ died for us" (Rom 5:8).

Jesus didn't wait. He pursued the Samaritan woman's heart in the same way he still pursues ours. So, the question is, What (if anything) are you waiting for, and why?

RELATED FACT

We are told the Samaritan woman heads to the well at noon or "the sixth hour," as some translations read. Several saints and scholars have offered that she went at the hottest part of the day because the well would be almost vacant at that time, hinting that due to the woman's romantic and marital history she wanted to avoid interaction with the gossiping locals.

BEHIND THE SCENES

This gospel story is said to have taken place at "Jacob's well" (Jn 4:6). Interestingly, this well is not explicitly mentioned anywhere in the Old Testament except to say that Jacob purchased land and erected an altar on it (see Genesis 33:19–20); the assumption is that the well would have naturally followed.

Tradition tells us that the well is likely located in central Samaria, near Mount Gerizim. The supposed well (if it is, in fact, Jacob's original site) still exists today and is roughly nine feet in diameter and about seventy-five feet deep, though in Jacob's and Jesus's time it would have been even deeper. Culturally speaking, wells were popular meeting and gathering places in the Mediterranean world where conversations, gossip, and courting would often take place. In fact, Moses, Isaac, and Jacob all met their eventual wives beside wells.

WORD PLAY

Reading through the conversation in the gospel is fascinating when you pay attention to the titles the Samaritan woman uses to address Jesus. First, she addresses him as "*Sir*" (Jn 4:11,15). Next, she calls Jesus a "*prophet*" (4:19). Almost immediately after that she proclaims that Jesus is, indeed, "*the Christ*" (4:29); and, finally, this faithful

woman declares him *"the Savior of the world"* (4:42)! The woman mirrors many of us as we come to know and understand Christ's identity more deeply over time through our encounter(s) with him.

JOURNAL

1. What is holding you back from accepting Christ's love and redemption? Is it pride or shame or sin? Do you refuse to forgive yourself for a sin you've already confessed, perhaps? Explain.

2. In order for us to completely surrender, we must hand over everything we have. How is God calling you to give what you have to him? Do you trust that he will take care of those things?

3. How can you identify with the woman at the well?

4. How is God pursuing your heart? How can you be open to his pursuit?

CHALLENGE FOR THE WEEK

Every day this week, say the words, "Jesus, I trust in you," five times in a row. These five words are so powerful. Say them with meaning and sincerity. Really think about what you are saying and truly mean it.

Fear No Evil

Fourth Sunday of Lent

OPENING PRAYER

Come, Holy Spirit. Flood my heart. Lead me closer to the Father, the Good Shepherd. God, thank you for always watching over me. I know you will always provide for me. Through your generosity, I will never be found wanting. Today, help me to reflect on your path for me. Sometimes I'm not sure where you have me at that very moment, but I always know where you are leading me: to you. Amen.

> **First Reading:** 1 Samuel 16:1b, 6–7, 10–13a
> **Responsorial Psalm:** Psalm 23:1–3a, 3b–4, 5, 6
> **Second Reading:** Ephesians 5:8–14
> **Gospel:** John 9:1–41

BEYOND WORDS

For what purpose were you created? What vocation did God place within you to fulfill?

Many of us walk through life in darkness, unable to answer either of the previous questions. Once we come to know God as Father through our Baptism and begin to seek and discern his will for our lives, the darkness fades away and we walk in the light. St. Paul illuminates (no pun intended) this point beautifully for the Ephesians in this week's second reading. For just as the man born blind only finally "sees" thanks to Christ in the gospel passage, we only come to understand life's purpose and our role within God's plan of salvation by way of Christ and his sacraments. Just as the miraculous healing of Christ points us to our Baptism, David's anointing in the first reading also has an almost sacramental feel to it. While Confirmation did not exist in its current understanding in the time of David, the anointing with oil and "the spirit of the Lord" rushing upon the young man certainly has sacramental undertones and foreshadowing.

While you may not yet fully comprehend what your future holds—what you are to do or who you are to become—the great news, as echoed in the psalm, is that you have nothing to fear. If you know, love, and serve God, he will be with you, at your side, to go before you and cast his light into all darkness. You need not fear; you need only say yes. God's plan for you is perfect and far better than anything you could ever come up with on your own.

RELATED FACT

St. John tells us that Jesus's spit mixed with the dirt forms "clay," which is then placed upon the blind man's eyes. Not coincidentally, what was used in Genesis by God to form and breathe life into the first man? Clay. This healing is more than a cool party trick but a rebirth, a baptism of sorts; the man has become a new creation in Christ.

BEHIND THE SCENES

Many have a tendency to look at scripture stories as either strictly symbolic or strictly historical, but to put them into just one category is short-sighted and intrinsically flawed. While there are varying ways to read and interpret scripture, several stories—like this week's gospel—are simultaneously historical and factual while also symbolic and analogical.

Nonbiblical Jewish and Roman writers and historians attest to the fact that there was a wonder worker from Nazareth—an itinerant preacher—who had a large following and reportedly worked miracles and healings, like opening the eyes of the blind, which no one could mirror or explain. Historically speaking, we have eyewitness testimony that Christ healed the blind, which puts this story in a literal, historical light (also, no pun intended).

Taking an even deeper, sacramental look (as St. John always invites us to do), however, we see (this pun very much intended) in the blind man something even more amazing. This is a story of baptism. The man born blind encounters God. The water that comes

from God is used to destroy the darkness, remove his blindness, and usher him into the light of life, just like Baptism removes our original sin. When he washes in the pool of "the one Sent," he can see, and he goes forth to bear witness to the truth he has experienced. So this story functions on both a historical and a symbolic/sacramental level, simultaneously.

WORD PLAY

Bethlehem was a small village about five miles south of Jerusalem. The hometown of Ruth's husband, Boaz, and their great-grandson King David (and his family), Bethlehem comes from a Hebrew phrase literally meaning "House of Bread." A fitting name for the city that also served as the birthplace of Jesus, our Bread of Life.

JOURNAL

1. How has your life changed since your Confirmation?

2. Do you feel as if you're walking around in the dark at times? How can you let Christ's light shine in and through you more perfectly?

3. When was a time that God provided for all your wants in a situation? What did that teach you about him?

CHALLENGE FOR THE WEEK

Read a passage from scripture that encourages you not to fear every day this week. Reflect on what you're afraid of, and find comfort in God's aid.

Dead Man Walking

Fifth Sunday of Lent

OPENING PRAYER

Jesus, you save me. You have lifted me out of the water when I have not trusted, you have cleansed me from my sin, and you have raised me from death. You are my only. I praise your name, for you alone are worthy. Help me to not be blinded by flesh, but to see with the spirit. Amen.

> **First Reading:** Ezekiel 37:12–14
> **Responsorial Psalm:** Psalm 130:1–8
> **Second Reading:** Romans 8:8–11
> **Gospel:** John 11:1–45

BEYOND WORDS

People had been waiting for the Messiah to come for centuries. In fact, many "messiahs" had come over the years claiming to be "the (anointed) one" of God. Of course, none of them were. None of them fulfilled the prophecies. None of them spoke like Christ spoke or could do what Jesus did. Even when Jesus came, proclaiming and working miracles, many *still refused* to believe. Many still do.

The prophet Ezekiel (in the first reading) told us, centuries before Jesus, that God would raise people from the grave. When Jesus literally raised Lazarus from the grave after four days, some saw the fulfillment of an age-old prophecy, but some still did not. Some were still "in the flesh" but not functioning or living in "the spirit," as St. Paul drew the comparison in his Letter to the Romans in the second reading. If we are trapped in sin and self and slaves to our pride, we will have a hard time believing even if a corpse should arise from his own grave before our own eyes!

It's no secret that many people today don't believe in God and that many who do believe in a "higher power" don't believe Jesus is the Messiah, the Christ. Given what you have seen and experienced, heard and know, do you believe? If you do, these last couple weeks of Lent really speak to your soul. If you aren't sure or do not believe that Jesus is the Savior whom God sent to save us, now is a good time to take it to prayer and get to Confession if you haven't been. For those enslaved to the flesh cannot live and "see" in the Spirit. Christ is the Resurrection and the *Life* who came to save us from sin, which is death.

RELATED FACT

"Jesus wept" (Jn 11:35) is the shortest verse in all of scripture.

BEHIND THE SCENES

Jesus's response to the news of his critically sick friend is a little puzzling on the surface. If the condition of Lazarus was so dire, why did Jesus wait two full days before making his way to Bethany?

Jesus allows (or chooses) the delay to his travel to help Lazarus, not out of chance, but with intentionality. Here we see Jesus's plan to grow everyone in faith, including his own apostles. Restoring a sick man—while impressive—cannot compare to raising a dead man. Christ has every intention of using this perceived "end" of death as a "means" of teaching about life eternal and God's power and sovereignty over both.

The language, too, about Lazarus being "asleep" was seemingly confusing to the disciples. The term *asleep* was a popular euphemism at the time and in scripture to describe actual death, but Jesus's followers, knowing him to be capable of anything and filled with the wisdom of God, thought that perhaps Lazarus was not completely dead. Jesus clarified that Lazarus was, indeed, dead to leave no doubt to them or us that what he was about to do was something no mere doctor or magician ever could.

WORD PLAY

Bethany is a small village a few miles east of Jerusalem where Mary and Martha lived along with their brother, Lazarus—until Lazarus died. Of course (spoiler alert) Jesus raised him and then all three lived together again. Scholars debate what *Bethany* means. Some say it means "House of Figs," and others offer a quite different "House of Affliction" or "House of Misery." Incidentally, the name *Lazarus* means "God has helped," which, in truth, seems like one of the greatest understatements of the gospels.

JOURNAL

1. In what ways do you still live "in the flesh"? Why would you want to live in the spirit instead of the flesh in the first place?

2. How can you grow in virtue to start living in the spirit? Read spiritual books? Go to daily Mass? Stay away from temptation?

3. Do you trust that Jesus is your Savior who died for you? If not, why?

CHALLENGE FOR THE WEEK

Carve half an hour out of a day this week to read the Gospel of Luke chapters 22 to 24. Read them carefully, visualizing the passage. Understand what Jesus did for you: facing public humiliation, physical injury, and death. Know that this was done in pure love for you.

The Way of the Cross
Palm Sunday

OPENING PRAYER

My God, sometimes I feel as if you've abandoned me. My cross seems too heavy to bear, but I continue to walk on because I know you will redeem this moment. Today, open my heart as I realize you must've felt the same way as you carried your Cross, walking to your death on Calvary. It was excruciating, but you did not give up out of love for me. As I face my personal crucifixion, help me to hope for the Resurrection. Amen.

> **Procession:** Matthew 21:1–11
> **First Reading:** Isaiah 50:4–7
> **Responsorial Psalm:** Psalm 22:8–9, 17–20, 23–24
> **Second Reading:** Philippians 2:6–11
> **Gospel:** Matthew 26:14–27:66

BEYOND WORDS

This story has been told countless times throughout the last two thousand years. You've heard it read and you've seen it portrayed on television and in films. Perhaps this year, before Palm Sunday Mass, you really work through each of these five readings (listed above) in your own Bible.

Highlight, underline, or journal about the words and phrases that really jump out at you. Spend time in prayer asking the Spirit "why" those words and phrases struck you at this point of your faith journey or this year, in particular. Put yourself into the Passion narrative. Find yourself in each scene from the upper room to the Garden of Gethsemane to Calvary. Where are you in proximity to the action? What does each place sound like, smell like, and look like?

This year, allow God to love you at each stop of the Passion, and renew your love for him through the sacrifice of your time and through your prayer.

RELATED FACT

We hear that during Jesus's mock trial before the Sanhedrin the high priest "tore his robes." Far more than an overdramatic gesture to make a point, it was a practice done to communicate extreme distress. The Law of Moses forbade a priest to tear their garments as they were sacred, and this action was done as a response to the supposed "blasphemy" from Jesus's claim.

BEHIND THE SCENES

Upon first glance or hearing, it may seem as though Jesus is angry with God upon the Cross, proclaiming, "My God, my God, why have you forsaken me?" In truth, however, this proclamation points us to a much deeper meaning that is not apparent to most listening. Jesus is actually quoting Psalm 22 here and, in echoing the first verse, is citing not just it but the entire psalm, which is the story of the righteous man who is suffering. Read through the length of Psalm 22 on your own.

In this psalm, we see the eventual vindication of the Suffering Servant and see that Jesus is putting his own suffering into context. Our Lord understands what is happening and how it all fits together in the "big picture" of salvation. As Jesus entrusts his suffering and death to his Father in heaven, we see not only the love and the trust but the fulfillment of God's promise and ultimate victory over sin, death, and the enemy.

WORD PLAY

Gethsemane was more than just a garden on the side of the Mount of Olives. Gethsemane was the location of the oil press, where olives were pressed or "squeezed" to emit their valuable oil. Hebrew in origin, *Gethsemane* is translated to "oil press" or, more to the point,

"crushing place," which is not an ironic title for the location where our Lord sweat blood.

JOURNAL

1. Jesus gives the disciples his Body and Blood at the Last Supper, and he gives it to you every Mass. What do you think about during the Liturgy of the Eucharist? Could you do a better job of focusing on who you're about to receive?

2. Jesus knew Peter would deny him three times, yet he still chose Peter to be the rock of the Church. What does this tell you about God's willingness to see us as what we could be, rather than through the lens of our failures? How does this make you feel?

3. In the Garden of Gethsemane, Jesus acknowledges this is difficult but still surrenders to God's will. How can you imitate this practice in your own life?

CHALLENGE FOR THE WEEK

Pray through the Stations of the Cross this week. You can do it on your own in a chapel, or you can look online to find a service near you. Meditate on what Christ endured and why. If you want to try something a little different, look online to find reflections for the stations through the eyes of Mary.

EASTER

Risen from the Dead

Easter Sunday

OPENING PRAYER

Jesus, you could never receive enough praise for your selfless love for me. You walked through death and came out victorious. Your name alone is worthy of praise. Open my heart to your Word. Guide me in the path you have set for me. Help me keep my eyes on you. Amen.

> **First Reading:** Acts 10:34a, 37–43
> **Responsorial Psalm:** Psalm 118:1–2, 16–17, 22–23
> **Second Reading:** Colossians 3:1–4 or 1 Corinthians 5:6b–8
> **Gospel:** John 20:1–9

BEYOND WORDS

So why did Jesus have to suffer and die?

I mean, couldn't God have done all this—won our salvation for us—some other, less gruesome, less painful way? Why did Christ have to endure suffering unto death? Why the thorns? Why the disfigured body and all the blood loss? Why the tomb and the darkness and the tears? Why did God have to die?

And why are we focusing on these themes, yet again, on Easter when we are supposed to be rejoicing? Why would the first reading recount what happened before the Resurrection? Why does the second reading then shift gears and tell us to look ahead and not back?

The answer is in the gospel: "For as yet they did not know the scripture, that he must rise from the dead" (Jn 20:9). Sin is death. We broke the covenant. God had to hatch a plan to cover the consequence of sin without losing us. So God became the plan. If he had merely dismissed it without consequence, God's Word would not be trustworthy, his plan would have been imperfect, and justice would not have been served.

Instead, God used death to defeat death and ensure our life. Suffering often comes with sin but ultimately reveals authentic love. The thorns of Good Friday make the roses of the garden tomb that much sweeter. The disfigured body gives way to our transfigured bodies in glory. The reason Easter Sunday is so sweet is precisely because Good Friday is so bitter. Jesus *had to rise from the dead* to pay our ransom and secure our salvation. This is not just good news; it is great news and deserves an *Alleluia* only after we realize the magnitude of this reality. Praise be to God!

RELATED FACT

In this week's Easter gospel, we are given the story of the Resurrection from "the disciple whom Jesus loved." Early scriptural tradition tells us that St. John Zebedee was this "mysterious" disciple, Jesus's closest friend, and the one he entrusted with the care of the Blessed Virgin Mary. Note the tone of brotherly competition that comes through in the story recounting that St. John and St. Peter chase one another to the tomb. The younger saint, John, points out not once, not twice, but three times that he beat our first pope in the foot race (see John 20:4, 6, 8).

BEHIND THE SCENES

As Catholics we profess and proclaim that we believe in "the resurrection of the body" in our Creed. Many people are somewhat confused, however, as to what this really means and all it entails and promises.

In 1 Corinthians 15, St. Paul reminds and assures us that we, too, will be raised and glorified in the image of Christ, who rose before us. Our Church teaches, with clarity, that one day our bodies and souls will be reunited at Christ's Second Coming, immediately preceding the last judgment. While we will be reunited with our own original body we had on Earth, it will be in a glorified form with new spiritual attributes and qualities. Our heavenly bodies will be similar to Christ's glorified body, which is why St. Paul tells the Colossians

that we "will appear with him in glory." You can read more about the resurrection of the body in the *Catechism* paragraphs 988–1013.

WORD PLAY

Worshipping on the "first day of the week" might naturally occur to us as meaning Sunday but to a Jew from Jesus's time, they would have viewed the calendar a bit differently. The *Sabbath* had always been the day of rest and worship, designed to stand alone and be set apart, marked by prayer and inactivity. The Sabbath in Jesus's time was celebrated. Following the Resurrection appearances and dawn of the early Church, however, we see thousands of Jews almost instantly stop meeting and worshipping on Saturdays. They began to gather for prayer and fellowship on Sundays, marking it not only as the first day of the week but as a memorial of the factual and historical Resurrection. A change in worship pattern of this magnitude would have been incredibly significant and only further points to the Resurrection of Jesus Christ as a historical fact.

JOURNAL

1. Take a minute to look back on Lent. How well did you prepare for the coming of Christ this year? In what areas did you do well? What areas do you need to work on to be more prepared next year?

2. Easter is about joy. What on this Earth makes you the most joyful? Time with family? A sports team? A good book? Being with a certain person? Why?

CHALLENGE FOR THE WEEK

Easter is a time of feasting, not fasting. Do something this week that makes you truly joyful. Whether that is reading a book in a windowsill, taking a long lunch, drinks with friends, walking or hiking, or being with family, do something that makes you thrive. Glorify God in whatever you do by thanking him for the peace and joy you experience.

His Mercy Endures Forever

Divine Mercy Sunday

OPENING PRAYER

O Good Jesus, I've doubted like Thomas so often, but, in your generosity, you continue to pursue me. All you desire from me is my heart. Lord, I believe. Help my unbelief. Even when I cannot see you, God, I know that you are with me. Send your Holy Spirit upon me to guide me and equip me to guide others closer to you. Amen.

> **First Reading:** Acts 2:42–47
> **Responsorial Psalm:** Psalm 118:2–4, 13–15, 22–24
> **Second Reading:** 1 Peter 1:3–9
> **Gospel:** John 20:19–31

BEYOND WORDS

Have you ever sat down to watch a movie or opened a book but already knew the ending? A mystery isn't nearly as fun if you begin the journey knowing "who did it." A thriller isn't nearly as thrilling if you know at the beginning who survives in the end. One of the great benefits, but also detractions, from really appreciating the Resurrection narratives and stories of the early Church in Acts is that we have two thousand years of knowing "what is going to happen next." The drama for our ancestors in the faith, however, is that they had no clue what was to come.

Why were the doors *still* locked on that Sunday, a week *after* the Resurrection? They were still in danger and didn't know what to do! Why was Thomas not there a week earlier? He had no idea Jesus was going to rise. Why did the first Christians gather together "to break bread," as we hear about in the first reading? Because they were learning how to live and worship as Christians and not, merely, as Jews. Why is St. Peter praising the followers who "without having

seen him [Jesus] love him" (1 Pet 1:8)? Because as the Church grew, more and more Christians had never actually met the Lord.

They didn't know how it was all going to end for them: perhaps martyrdom, old age, or more Roman upheaval. They had no clue except to trust in God and in his mercy. They had to be present to what they "knew," and the other apostles knew Christ had risen. Imagine how Thomas must have felt to actually see the wounds. It's that kind of eyewitness encounter that gives you the courage to leave your home, native land, and extended family and go out to baptize the nations, bear witness to the Gospel, and, eventually, spill your own blood for the sake of it.

RELATED FACT

The final line of the second reading from 1 Peter states what the "goal" of the faith is for each one of us. Why do we study scripture, pray, go to Mass, or get involved in the Church? The answer is *salvation*—yours and everyone's. Go back and read 1 Peter 1:9 and commit it to memory.

BEHIND THE SCENES

Scholars debate whether or not St. John—the beloved disciple—is *really* the one who wrote his gospel or if it was written by one of St. John's disciples. Regardless of who actually put the pen to paper, it's commonly held that St. John's gospel was the final of the four written. Several of the stories included in John's gospel are unique to it: the wedding feast at Cana, the Samaritan woman at the well, the Bread of Life discourse, the washing of the feet, the extended dialogue with Pontius Pilate, the words to Mary from the Cross, and the Resurrection appearance beside Galilee (Tiberias), just to name a few. Many believe that St. John knew about the other gospels circulating and added his only later to "fill in" a few gaps, offering specific and intentional stories to further strengthen and solidify the early Church followers and practices.

Pay attention, in particular, to the final verse of his gospel, which reads, "But there are also many other things which Jesus did; were

every one of them to be written, I suppose that the world itself could not contain the books that would be written" (Jn 21:25). This verse not only offers valuable insight into the fact that eyewitnesses (like the apostles) had countless more stories not inspired by the Holy Spirit to share and record. By extension, it shows that the oral tradition of the early Church was seen as a vital source of Christian truth.

WORD PLAY

We hear in the gospel that Jesus "*breathed*" on them. The Greek word *inspirare* means "to breathe into." Just as in Eden when God breathed life into the dust to bring life to Adam, here we see God breathing new life into and upon his apostles. Just as the Holy Spirit inspired the sacred scriptures by breathing through the pens of men, the Spirit will now breathe through our apostles for the forgiveness of sins.

JOURNAL

1. Jesus enters the room and wishes peace unto the disciples. He wishes peace for you, too. Do you feel the peace of Christ? Why or why not?

2. The disciples were still in hiding in the upper room a week after Jesus appeared to them. Have you ever felt afraid to do the right thing? How can the Holy Spirit give you the courage to overcome that fear?

3. Have you ever been challenged about your faith? What inspires you to believe, even when others tell you not to?

4. Have you ever contemplated that Jesus had the Bible written just so that you could know him? Do you take advantage of this incredible gift?

CHALLENGE FOR THE WEEK

Learn about a Eucharistic miracle, and thank God for providing so many ways to inspire your belief.

Their Eyes Were Opened

Third Sunday of Easter

OPENING PRAYER

Jesus, you are holy and you know me. You come to me; you pursue me. You know the depths of my heart, and only you can open it to receive your ever-flowing love. Help me to recognize your voice. Help me to see your face. Help me to be so familiar with you that I can hear you clearly in a full crowd. Amen.

> **First Reading:** Acts 2:14, 22–33
> **Responsorial Psalm:** Psalm 16:1–2, 5, 7–11
> **Second Reading:** 1 Peter 1:17–21
> **Gospel:** Luke 24:13–35

BEYOND WORDS

People learn differently. Think back to high school or college. Some took notes diligently, while others just stared at the board and listened intently. Some minds retain by repetition and others by exposition. Some people can recall facts, and others can only learn through experience. One of the greatest common denominators, however, in effective teaching methods—both past and present—is the use of stories. No matter how artistic or analytical a listener might be, a well-told story is a timeless way of making (and retaining) a teaching point.

In this week's readings, we have three different types of "stories," if you will. In the first reading, St. Peter is delivering eyewitness testimony of the ministry of Jesus Christ to old followers and new believers alike. He is recounting past events and prophecies and putting them into a new context, encapsulating all that Jesus did in just a few short verses. In the second reading, St. Peter, again, is bearing witness to Christ's life and work but in a much wider historical context. Rather than sharing glory stories about their days together on Earth,

our first pope is demonstrating (historically and philosophically) how Jesus was always the Father's plan of salvation for us. But rather than boring us with details, he frames this history lesson as a story.

Finally, in the gospel, we have one of the most compelling stories in all the gospels, the famous "Road to Emmaus" story. Here, the Holy Spirit works through St. Luke to share a story that is historically true but, also, symbolically rich. Christ himself draws near and asks the travelers about their "story," if you will. After listening, Jesus then weaves together story after story from the Torah and the prophets, all the while walking them to the Eucharistic table. This encounter not only prefigures our Mass (scripture and sacrament shared on a Sunday) but also equips the two travelers with—what?—a story for the ages.

When we slow down long enough to look at our lives and how God is present and has always been, we begin to see how he connects the dots between the stories of our lives and others' journeys, as well. The stories begin and end in him and at his altar.

RELATED FACT

The exact location of Emmaus is actually a bit of a mystery for modern scholars and archaeologists. While the gospel places it roughly sixty *stadia* (or seven miles) west of Jerusalem, no village by that name at that distance survived over the centuries. There are two locations for Emmaus considered plausible, but each are more ten miles away from Jerusalem.

BEHIND THE SCENES

On the road to Emmaus, we see the two disciples downtrodden because they were hoping that Jesus "would be the one to redeem Israel" (Lk 24:21). Following the Crucifixion, those who had closely followed Jesus were saddened, believing that his death meant he was not, actually, the Messiah who was promised by God and foretold in prophecy. Expecting a military leader who would overthrow the Roman Empire and end the oppression of God's Chosen People

(Israel), the disciples were distraught to see the seeming powerlessness of Christ upon the Cross. Prevented from recognizing Jesus—until the Eucharistic breaking of the bread—the disciples, first, had the pleasure of hearing how the messianic prophecies foretold what would happen with and to Jesus. It was only after being enlightened by the Word that their souls would be nourished by the Body and Blood, just like our modern Mass, when the Messiah still comes to nourish our minds, bodies, and souls.

WORD PLAY

The word *ransomed* that we hear in the second reading from 1 Peter is derived from *redemptio*, meaning "deliverance" or "releasing." We were released and delivered from our futile conduct by the Blood of Christ's Cross.

JOURNAL

1. If God were to ask you to share the story of how you came to know him, what would you say?

2. If God was speaking in a crowd and you passed by, would you be able to "recognize" his voice? How can you become more familiar with him?

CHALLENGE FOR THE WEEK

Silence can be an intimidating thing. Why do you think our first instinct when faced with silence is to grab our phone? However, silence is one way we can hear and become familiar with Jesus's voice. Every day this week, spend five full minutes in silence. Put your phone and any other distractions away. This should be done in a quiet room or, better yet, in Eucharistic Adoration. Allow the Lord to speak to you. Do not say anything. Remain still and listen.

Fear No Evil

Fourth Sunday of Easter

OPENING PRAYER

Loving Father, give me the grace to trust you in all things. I know in my heart that you love me and will always take care of me, but sometimes fear and worry make it hard for my head to believe that. Give me the courage to become the person you are calling me to be, fully trusting that you will accompany me on this journey. You are the Good Shepherd, and I am safe in your loving arms. Help me to understand this truth as I read your Word today. Amen.

> **First Reading:** Acts 2:14a, 36–41
> **Responsorial Psalm:** Psalm 23:1–6
> **Second Reading:** 1 Peter 2:20b–25
> **Gospel:** John 10:1–10

BEYOND WORDS

Were you ever home alone and you heard a strange sound? Especially when you were younger, the darkness and the unknown had a way of becoming even scarier when there was no one else in the house.

It's said that there is strength in numbers, so it is no wonder why solitude can make someone feel "uneasy" about the potential dangers that lurk around them.

Shepherds knew well the dangers around them. Shepherds didn't have an easy life. While they sometimes hung out in the hills in groups, they were often alone with their sheep. Constantly keeping watch for threats to their flock, surveying the landscape for wandering sheep making a break for greener pastures, and even traversing treacherous terrain to rescue those who had gone missing left shepherds with no one but their sheep. The gospel tells us what a Good Shepherd we have in Jesus, who laid down his life for us, his flock. The second reading reminds us that Christ laid down his life because

we, the sheep, had gone astray. This week's psalm—one of (if not) the most famous of all the psalms—paints a picture of a "sheep" keenly aware that, even though he is alone, with the Lord as his Shepherd he is never alone.

St. Peter was assuredly not alone during this, his first great sermon, that we hear in the first reading from Acts. What is it, you may ask, that turns a fisherman into our first shepherd, our first pope? His awareness that God was with him and that, no matter what evil befell him, Peter need not fear, because God is the true Shepherd.

RELATED FACT

The shepherd's "rod and staff" were of tremendous importance to his daily herding duties. The rod was used to defend the shepherd and his flock from wild animals or snakes, while also being used to discipline sheep when necessary. The staff offered support, allowing the shepherd to lean on it when tired, but—given its crooked end—also served as a way for the shepherd to draw sheep near to him. The rod symbolizes authority while the staff represents comfort.

BEHIND THE SCENES

In the passage from John 10 regarding the shepherd and the sheep, we hear Jesus reveal himself as "the gate" or the door, depending on the translation (Jn 10:9). In the verse immediately following this week's gospel (10:11), we hear Christ refer to himself as "the Good Shepherd."

The close proximity might almost sound like our Lord is mixing metaphors. So, which is it? Is Jesus the gate or the shepherd? Actually, in this case, Christ is both. Oftentimes in the hills while guarding their sheep, shepherds would create small enclosures using mud or branches to corral sheep at night. In an effort to ensure their safety from wild animals or thieves, the "good" shepherd (who cared about his sheep) would lie down in the opening of the enclosure, acting as a sort of human gate. No one and nothing got in or out without

going through the shepherd. Because we are the sheep and Christ is the Good Shepherd, there's no better place to be than in his fold.

WORD PLAY

The word *exhort* used to describe St. Peter in the first reading from Acts is from the Latin *exhortari*, meaning "to thoroughly encourage."

JOURNAL

1. When Jesus said he came so that we could "have life and have it more abundantly," what do you think he meant?

2. Like a sheep safe in the shepherd's arms, do you allow yourself to be held by the Lord? Or do you push him away?

3. What "thieves" (threats) are you afraid will come and do damage to your life? How can Christ help you overcome these fears?

4. Is it hard to hear God's voice? Why?

CHALLENGE FOR THE WEEK

Go into a chapel and spend fifteen minutes in silence, with a clear head. If you start thinking about something, start the fifteen minutes over. Relax by repeating a simple truth such as "Jesus, I trust in you," "Come, Holy Spirit," or "You are the King of Kings." When your heart is silent, it's easier to hear the Lord.

Do the Works that He Did

Fifth Sunday of Easter

OPENING PRAYER

Jesus, you are the Way, the Truth, and the Life. You call me to be in union with you because you are my true joy. Help me accept you and your Word. Give me the grace to understand your teachings and how to thrive in this life. Amen.

> **First Reading:** Acts 6:1–7
> **Responsorial Psalm:** Psalm 33:1–2, 4–5, 18–19
> **Second Reading:** 1 Peter 2:4–9
> **Gospel:** John 14:1–12

BEYOND WORDS

St. Augustine once wrote, "If you believe what you like in the gospels, and reject what you don't like, it is not the gospel you believe, but yourself." He could just as easily have written that sentence in the twenty-first century as he did in the fifth century. We live in a culture where people often pick and choose and justify what they believe to be truth. The problem, as we see in this week's gospel, is that Christ clearly proclaims that he—and he alone is—"*the* way, and *the* truth, and *the* life" (Jn 14:6). Put simply, the Bread of Life is not one option in the Catholic cafeteria for those truly seeking truth; he is the only option.

Jesus put it plainly: if we truly believe in him, we'll do the works that he did. The second reading reminds us what happens to those who live and preach like Christ: rejection. It goes on to remind us, though, of how heroic and beautiful a call we have in Christ, that we are chosen and royal and set apart for this great mission. The Church needs faithful witnesses to safeguard and proclaim Christ's truth to the greater world. This call gave way to the first deacons that we hear about in the first reading. Souls are hungry for the truth of Christ.

The question, still today, is whether those who know Jesus are willing to do anything about it.

RELATED FACT

The word *Hellenists* in the first reading from Acts has a tendency to throw people a bit. Hellenists were a faction of Greeks that were immersed in their own Greek culture and whose desire was to insert Greek culture into every facet of life. In essence, to "Hellenize" a group was to try to get them to adapt everything Greek, from the language to the religious practices to the food, and so on.

BEHIND THE SCENES

This week's gospel passage offers us an intriguing look at what heaven is like when Jesus tells us, "In my Father's house are many rooms" (Jn 14:2). Upon hearing this, our natural mindset in the West is to think of heaven as sort of a huge mansion where everyone has their own presidential suite. It's as though Jesus is promising us something of a five-star, spa-like existence for eternity.

Well, yes and no.

In the time of Jesus there was a common practice during the betrothal process. Once betrothed (which we previously discussed in Advent), but before living together, a couple had to go through a period of preparation time. While the bride prepared herself for their life together and to leave her family home, the groom went off to his father's house and began working on a suitable wedding home for him and his new wife. The new dwelling place was commonly its own quarters within the larger familial home (sort of like a guest room), or its own structure if the resources were available. Interestingly, it was only when the father of the groom said the wedding chamber was ready that the groom could then seek his bride and bring her home to seal their covenant and consummate their relationship.

Throughout scripture, God uses the analogy of Christ as the bridegroom and the Church as the bride to describe his unyielding and intimate love for his people. Jesus employs this imagery to

explain to us that heaven is far more than a mansion but, rather, the greatest possible intimacy rooted in perfect and sacrificial love.

WORD PLAY

The word *deacon* comes from the Greek word *diakonos*, meaning "servant." We see the first deacons called into service in Acts chapter 6; they were expected to be men of good reputation and filled with the Spirit and wisdom.

JOURNAL

1. What Church teachings do you struggle with? Why?

2. What questions do you have about those teachings that, if answered, would bring you clarity?

3. In what ways can you open your heart to God's teachings?

CHALLENGE FOR THE WEEK

This week, pick one teaching you struggle with and do research on it. Look up answers to your questions. Learn about what the teaching truly is, what it says, and why the Church teaches it. As you are doing this, ask God for clarity and an open mind.

Hope Fully

Sixth Sunday of Easter

OPENING PRAYER

Come, Holy Spirit. Ignite my heart with the love of Christ. Give me the right words to share my faith with others. Thank you for always working on my behalf. I know that so long as my hope is in Christ, I have nothing to fear. The Lord will remain faithful to his promises. Holy Spirit, inspire me to accept the wisdom found in today's readings. Amen.

> **First Reading:** Acts 8:5–8, 14–17
> **Responsorial Psalm:** Psalm 66:1–7, 16, 20
> **Second Reading:** 1 Peter 3:15–18
> **Gospel:** John 14:15–21

BEYOND WORDS

The news can be really depressing. Terrorist attacks, racial unrest, widespread abortion, human trafficking, political unrest, economic instability, the pornography pandemic—these are just a few examples of how our modern culture seems to be crumbling before our very eyes. So how does the modern Christian heart keep from becoming "jaded"? How do we become and remain a "resurrection people" with so much death and hopelessness around us?

We focus on the Resurrection. In fact, every Sunday is a mini-Easter in which God offers us a new and more hope-filled perspective on death and life. The gospel reminds us that God did not abandon us or leave us orphans. In fact, we are even more powerful than we could imagine because we have the Holy Spirit. God's Spirit is still just as available to us today as it was to those we hear about in the first reading. Miracles still happen. No earthly force can withstand the power of heaven. This is the reason St. Peter implores us not to lose our hope, as we hear in the second reading. He tell us not only

EASTER

99

to remain hopeful but to be prepared to tell people the reason for our hope: Jesus Christ. Note, too, that we are to tell people—to actively share our witness—with gentleness and reverence. Good words to keep in mind and a great challenge to take the next time we go to post on social media, huh?

RELATED FACT

You'll notice that Acts says, "Philip went *down* to a city of Samaria." Since the city of Jerusalem was built atop Mount Zion, leaving there to travel anywhere was always downhill. The region and the city of Samaria was a beautiful area filled with mountains and valleys, but all "lower" than Jerusalem in terms of altitude and sea level.

BEHIND THE SCENES

The scene in this week's first reading is one of the more intriguing episodes in Acts. We see Sts. Peter and John in Samaria—a place with long-standing tension toward the Jews—where the people there are amazingly demonstrating their belief in Christ and accepting the Word of God.

The line "that they might receive the Holy Spirit, for it had not yet fallen upon any of them," is puzzling to many modern Christians. How could those who had been baptized in the name of Jesus not have "received" the Holy Spirit yet or not had that reception fully animated?

The Church uses this episode as one example of the distinctions between the Sacraments of Baptism and Confirmation. While Baptism confers the Holy Spirit in more "invisible" ways, Confirmation unleashes the Spirit in more "visible" ways. Although deacons, then and now, can baptize us, we see Sts. Peter and John—who are bishops—laying on hands and conferring the Holy Spirit upon the people, just as modern bishops still do at our own Sacrament of Confirmation. This distinction is one example of how these two Sacraments of Initiation are complementary but separate, as witnessed with the souls in Samaria who had been initiated into the family

but had not yet fully realized the power and role of the Holy Spirit within them.

WORD PLAY

The title *Advocate* comes from the Latin *advocatus*, meaning "to call to one's aid." The root of the word is *vocare*—which is where we get the term *vocation*—and it means "to call."

JOURNAL

1. Are you confident of your hope in the Lord? Who might need to hear about the hope you have in Jesus, and why?

2. Who do you know who truly lets the Holy Spirit work through them? What are some of your favorite things about that person?

3. What does being a hopeful person look like? What does it feel like?

4. If someone didn't know you, would they be able to tell that you are a disciple of Jesus? How?

CHALLENGE FOR THE WEEK

The easiest way to rid our lives of hope is to be negative. As discussed earlier, it's really easy to be negative. Phrases like "Man, this weather is awful," slip out of our mouths almost unconsciously. This week, commit to being positive. This means (1) no complaining and (2) whenever something happens that makes you want to complain, offer it back to the Lord and trust that he has a purpose for the situation. You can do it!

Make Disciples of All Nations

Ascension of the Lord

OPENING PRAYER

God, you are everything I need. You are my strength when I am weak. Help me to be bold. Help me follow your call to make disciples. Give me the courage to go out in the world and spread your love. You are above all things, and I am grateful to serve you. Amen.

> **First Reading:** Acts 1:1–11
> **Responsorial Psalm:** Psalm 47:2–3, 6–9
> **Second Reading:** Ephesians 1:17–23
> **Gospel:** Matthew 28:16–20

BEYOND WORDS

If you're reading this, then it means you woke up this morning. If you woke up this morning, it means God has a mission for you today. It may be huge; it may be small. It may be frightening; it may be fun. It may challenge you to persevere, or it may push you to trust more deeply than ever before, but make no mistake, God has a mission for you that only you can fulfill.

Plenty of daily missions go unfulfilled. Many followers of Jesus are standing around, heads in the clouds (much like the apostles at the end of the first reading), wondering what to do next. The apostles had an excuse, as they had not yet received the Holy Spirit at Pentecost (that happens next week). You've been baptized, though. You've most likely been confirmed. You're not lacking in the Holy Spirit. So, what's your excuse? Are you out proclaiming Christ to the nations? Do others see your bold witness and seek the sacraments that bring you such confidence and joy? Have "the eyes of your hearts (been) enlightened," as St. Paul put it to the Ephesians in the second reading?

Either Christ rose or he didn't. Either Jesus ascended or he didn't. These are amazing truths that call us to an amazing response. All

God needs is your permission to make you a saint. A great adventure awaits you today, and your "yes" is all God needs. So will you accept the mission and get to work, or stand around staring at the sky?

RELATED FACT

Most scholars believe that "the mountain to which Jesus had directed them" (Mt 28:16) in this conclusion to St. Matthew's gospel is Mount Tabor, where the Transfiguration also occurred. The mountain that Jesus ascended from, however, is the Mount of Olives back down in Jerusalem.

BEHIND THE SCENES

In this final scene of St. Matthew's gospel, we see Jesus's story come full circle, at least geographically. In his ordering them back to Galilee, to the mountain location Christ had in mind, we notice a few important things. First, this is where Jesus's earthly mission "began" years earlier and will "end" (so to speak). It was in Galilee that Jesus grew up, where he first called the apostles, worked his first miracles, and announced that the forthcoming kingdom of God was now at hand. Next, just as so many important Old Testament and gospel events prior had taken place high atop a mountain, so this one, too, would offer a "heightened" perspective to his followers. It's important to note here, however, that while Jesus gave them the great commissioning here in Galilee atop Mount Tabor, our Lord ascended from the Mount of Olives.

In the same way that Jesus's earthly mission launched from Galilee, the apostles' new earthly mission will launch from the same location. We hear that the apostles worshipped, but some doubted (see Matthew 28:17). This may seem odd given that they've just spent forty days with the risen Lord working miracles and instructing them in the faith. But the Greek in Matthew doesn't say that *all* the apostles doubted, inferring instead that some doubted and some believed. This is understandable given their different experiences and points on their individual faith walks combined with the fact

that the Holy Spirit had yet to descend at Pentecost, illuminating their minds and hearts.

WORD PLAY

The word *auctor* is Latin for "author" and means "originator or promoter." The word *authority* comes from the Latin *auctoritas,* meaning "author's right."

JOURNAL

1. Do the people in your life easily realize you as Catholic? Why or why not?

2. In what ways are you following your baptismal call to "make disciples of all nations"?

3. What holds you back from spreading God's word?

4. Are you well equipped to spread God's message? Do you pray? Do you read the Bible? Do you know the lives of the saints?

5. How can you better equip yourself for this mission you are on?

CHALLENGE FOR THE WEEK

Talk to someone about God this week. It can be your coworker, a friend, or some random person that you meet at a coffee shop. Be bold. You do not have to get in a large debate about him, but casually talk about him with someone. See their point of view, ask them questions, and share your belief. This does not have to be a long conversation, but it is practice for your mission!

Ascension of the Lord

Seventh Sunday of Easter

OPENING PRAYER

Lord, in good times and in bad, in times of clarity and uncertainty, in times of joy and times of anxiety, you are with us. You are faithful, God, and your promises are trustworthy. Help me to trust in your perfect plan and perfect timing. Help me to be strong for you and in you and to glorify your name with my life. Amen.

> **First Reading:** Acts 1:12–14
> **Responsorial Psalm:** Psalm 27:1, 4, 7–8
> **Second Reading:** 1 Peter 4:13–16
> **Gospel:** John 17:1–11a

BEYOND WORDS

Both checkers and chess are games of strategy. Though the latter requires more forward thinking and strategy than the former, both games require that we pull back and take a broader vision of the playing board before us. Checkers and chess each offer us the challenge and gift of perspective.

Life is much the same way. We can often lose perspective and vision of the world around us, merely reacting to each situation. When we feel out of control or stressed we may have the tendency merely to act out rather than hold our tongue or turn to God in prayer. At the same time, it may also be our first inclination to systematically control everything before us. We may survey a situation and begin to look several moves ahead, predicting (or trying to control) what will happen down the line, and allow fear or anxiety or self-preservation to dictate our every move, even to our own detriment.

Then there's the Lord, the chess master, who holds all things together, encouraging and asking us to trust in his perfect plan, strategy, and timing. In the first reading, the remaining apostles had just watched Jesus ascend to heaven. The promised Holy Spirit had not yet fallen upon them. Rather than hatching a plan and strategy and creating actionable steps to mitigate damage and protect themselves from further Roman or Pharisees' threats, they prayed. They "devoted themselves" to prayer. They didn't know how this chess match was going to unfold, but they knew that prayer and discernment was their best course of action . . . before taking action. They, like the psalmist, believed that they would "see the good things of the Lord" in due time. Of course, they had also just seen their crucified Lord in his risen, glorified form for forty days prior to the Ascension. So they had a new perspective, one rooted in not only faithful confidence but also jubilant expectation. Seeing Christ in his glory offered them hope in their own sufferings. The apostles were not out of the proverbial woods yet—not even close! They were under persecution, as well, but the Resurrection and Christ's glory gave context to the sufferings they had and would endure.

It's for this reason that in the gospel, Jesus's words (though on the surface confusing) are so consoling. He speaks over and over about glorifying the Father and how that was the mission he had accepted and the role he'd fulfilled. In following Jesus today, we still bring glory to the Father, in Christ's image, but only if we keep a prayerful perspective. We must remain proactive and not reactive; we must not shy away from sufferings but—like Christ— embrace that which is placed before us and trust in God's timing and perfect plan. Rather than seizing a situation or attempting to control it, we let situations play out as we prayerfully discern the next step God is calling us to, not cowering, afraid to move, nor charging ahead according to our own plans. When we seek the Lord's glory rather than our own safety, comfort, or affirmation, God's will is done, God is glorified, and we, too, will taste the glory of heaven that awaits.

RELATED FACT

We hear "a sabbath day's journey" used as a measure of distance in this week's first reading from Acts. Jews were strictly forbidden under the Law of Moses to do any substantive work or travel on the Sabbath as

God (back in Genesis) had ordered and ordained the Sabbath to be a day of rest. As a result, "limits" were placed on what could and could not be lawfully done and distances placed on what was reasonable to travel without violating the command to enter into the Sabbath. A Jew was permitted to travel two thousand cubits on the Sabbath (see Exodus 16:29 and Numbers 35:5); a cubit measured about 1.5 feet. So two thousand cubits equated to roughly 1,000 yards or 3,000 feet (which is equal to just over a half of a mile). So even without visiting the Holy Land in person, one can ascertain from the reading the distance from Mount Olivet to Jerusalem using this idiomatic expression.

BEHIND THE SCENES

We hear that the eleven (remaining) apostles are gathered in the "upper room" as it is mentioned in the first reading from Acts. Also known as the "cenacle" (from the Latin *cenaculum*, a derivative of "cena" which means dinner), it was believed to be a "home base" of sorts for Jesus and his disciples when inside the holy city of Jerusalem, located just across the Kidron Valley and the Mount of Olives.

Most scholars agree the upper room/cenacle is the very same room where both the Last Supper occurred and where the Holy Spirit fell upon the Blessed Virgin Mary and the disciples on the Feast of Pentecost. Traditionally speaking, the site is believed to be the upstairs gathering space in the home of St. (John) Mark's mother. We see later in Acts after St. Peter's miraculous "jail break" (see Acts 12) that he immediately heads to a home where the inhabitants and, specifically, the maidservant, Rhoda, are familiar with him. If this was, indeed, the same site and St. Mark's mother the host, it would explain the early relationship and knowledge St. Peter had of the future gospel writer/evangelist and could be what prompted both him and, later, St. Paul to take Mark under their wing as a scribe and traveling companion.

WORD PLAY

When lists appear naming the twelve apostles, there are occasionally supposed discrepancies with some of the names. Upon a closer glance,

however, we see they are the same people though some go by different names. Bartholomew as listed here in Acts, for instance, also goes by the name Nathanael (in John's gospel). Likewise, just as we see "Judas, son of James" listed here, we also see this Judas listed as Jude (to avoid confusion with Judas Iscariot, the betrayer) or as Jude Thaddeus, again, to create distance between him and the fallen apostle.

JOURNAL

1. We all like to be recognized and affirmed. It's human nature. Sometimes, though, we can use the God-given gifts we are given to (un)intentionally lead others back to us rather than the Lord, the Giver of all good gifts. What are some ways or instances that you have used your talents or skills for your own attention and gain?

2. What are some practical and tangible ways you can use your gifts and talents to bring glory to the Lord?

3. Do you make it a point to rest on the Sabbath (Sunday) or do you fill it with activities? How might that affect your prayer life and relationship with God?

4. The second reading and gospel tell us that suffering is okay because ultimately it will glorify God. Are you able to think about the glory of God in moments of suffering? What can you do to bring glory to God in those moments?

CHALLENGE FOR THE WEEK

Look around your life at those areas where you are uncertain about the future or situations are out of your control. Now, every time you are anxious about a situation or relationship or how something will end or turn out this week, pause and offer an Our Father, praying and trusting that the Lord's will be done in every circumstance. No matter how many times a day you have to do it, create a habit to stop and pray where you otherwise want to control.

Filled with the Holy Spirit

Pentecost Sunday

OPENING PRAYER

Renew me, O God. Strip away the walls around my heart. Clean out the dusty corners I try to ignore. Heal the bruises and the cracks. Renew me, O God. For by your wounds, I live. I pray for a deeper understanding of this truth so that I may be convicted, with more fervor than ever before, to go out and share the Good News with others. Renew me, O good and gracious God. Amen.

> **(Mass during the Day)**
> **First Reading:** Acts 2:1–11
> **Responsorial Psalm:** Psalm 104:1, 24, 29–31, 34
> **Second Reading:** 1 Corinthians 12:3b–7, 12–13
> **Gospel:** John 20:19–23

BEYOND WORDS

Carousels are really exciting—for children. When you're a kid the carousel seems huge and exhilarating. You don't mind the monotony of the circle you're "riding" or the redundancy of the rising and falling motion. It's not until you become older and more mature that you see the carousel for what it is: safe and predictable. The roller coaster, on the other hand, is exhilarating and "dangerous." That shoulder harness or lap bar is the only thing holding you down, and you know it.

Now, which of these rides most directly resembles your faith life: the carousel or the roller coaster? Is your faith predictable or dangerous?

A life led by the Holy Spirit is exciting and "unsafe." As we see in the first reading, the apostles are on the verge of changing the world—all they are lacking is the power of God. Christians can and will renew the face of the Earth (see Psalm 104: 30), as the psalm says, and they have for centuries, wherever the Spirit has been allowed to work through

them. The Lord equips his Church with gifts (second reading), authority (gospel), and power (first reading) so that all would come to know God's love and mercy. Some believers opt for the safety and predictability of a carousel relationship with God, where they never truly surrender control. Pentecost invites us to jump in the roller-coaster car held together only by God's Love (whom we call the Holy Spirit), throw our hands in the air, and scream with joy each day of this great adventure we call life until he calls us home to heaven.

RELATED FACT

The cities listed in the end of the first reading from Acts are more than an amusing way to make the Sunday lector get tongue-tied or lose their mind. The cities listed, from "Parthians" through "Arabs," represent international visitors from throughout the Mediterranean world and beyond who have come to Jerusalem to worship. Many of these international travelers would go on to accept the Gospel and serve as a foreshadowing of how nations and believers around the globe would later hear the Gospel, accept it, and be reborn in Christ.

BEHIND THE SCENES

The Jewish people celebrated a number of "feasts" annually. These feasts were special celebrations established by God where the Jews could come together to experience and praise God in a special and specific way. The most significant feasts were the feast of Passover, the feast of Pentecost, and the feast of Tabernacles.

On the feast of Pentecost, the Jews celebrated a harvest festival (see Exodus 23:16) celebrating God's fidelity for the bounty he provided (through rain, crops, etc.). Additionally (and traditionally), the feast of Pentecost was also closely connected with the Jews receiving the Law of God through Moses atop Mount Sinai.

Just as God overshadowed and touched Earth in a powerful way atop Mount Sinai, offering truth to his children in an effort to draw all people to himself, now the Holy Spirit would overshadow and touch Earth with the power of God, yet again. The Holy Spirit who

will "guide you into all the truth" (Jn 16:13) descends not to the mountaintop but to the upper room, imparting powerful spiritual gifts upon the disciples gathered there, in order to empower them to fulfill their evangelistic mission.

WORD PLAY

The gospel tells us that Jesus "*breathed* on" his apostles. The word for "breathe" comes from the Latin *inspirare*, meaning "to breathe in(to)." It is said that the sacred scriptures, the sacraments, and the Church are all "inspired" by God, meaning that the Holy Spirit—this strong driving wind—is breathing his divine grace and life into each, propelling and impelling them to order God's children to the truth. Christ's disciples "breathe in" his grace and divine life, and we have inspiration that we can then turn and breathe out (respiration) that life onto all we encounter.

JOURNAL

1. God sent his Son to Earth to save souls. In the gospel, Jesus tells the disciples, "As the Father has sent me, even so I send you." How does this apply to your life?

2. What part of your life might need to be renewed (your religious education, your humility, your prayer life, etc.)?

3. What are some of your spiritual gifts?

4. Who is someone in your life that you could affirm for their spiritual gifts?

CHALLENGE FOR THE WEEK

The easy thing about prayer is that it gives us the opportunity to ask God to do his part. The challenging thing about life is that we have to do our part. Today, we pray to be renewed. This week follow that theme by actually trying something new! Whether it's ordering something different than your usual at lunch or trying a different type of prayer, you'll experience the fruit that comes from desiring to grow.

111

ORDINARY
TIME

Perfect Intimacy

Solemnity of the Most Holy Trinity

OPENING PRAYER

Lord God, you know me down to the number of hairs on my head, and you call me to a deep relationship with you. It is undeniable; you want me as your own. Help me accept your invitation. Allow me to be hidden within you. Amen.

> **First Reading:** Exodus 34:4b–6, 8–9
> **Responsorial Psalm:** Daniel 3:52–55
> **Second Reading:** 2 Corinthians 13:11–13
> **Gospel:** John 3:16–18

BEYOND WORDS

The world craves intimacy. Sadly, the word *intimate* has lost its proper connotation in modern culture. Real intimacy, at its core, is far more about the spirit than the flesh. From the Latin *intimus*, *intimate* means to "make the innermost known." The world craves a love that is completely trustworthy, safe, and true. To make our innermost hearts, fears, struggles, pains, and anxieties known to another is frightening because it can be taken advantage of and betrayed. Most heartbreak stems from a desire for intimacy that has been mishandled.

True prayer is intimate. The sacraments are intimate. The Holy Trinity offers us perfect intimacy because pure love can only give of itself and takes nothing in return. In this way, the Holy Trinity is, obviously, perfect intimacy because all three persons (and one God) are perfect love.

Today's first reading demonstrates God's desire for intimacy with us, which is why he came near to Moses and, incidentally, why he gave us the Ten Commandments—to keep us in right *relationship* with himself. St. Paul's second letter to the Corinthians not only demonstrates his deep, personal love for them but gives instruction on how they are to grow in holy intimacy with one another. God, in giving us his only Son to save us, demonstrated not only his love for Christ but his great love for us—his sinful but beloved children. God offers us himself in love and grace and fellowship. Humility accepts the proposal, while pride rejects it and him.

RELATED FACT

A holy kiss on the cheek was a common greeting in the Mediterranean world during Jesus's time. We see an example of this practice mentioned in Luke 7:45, a sign of peace. Do you remember the "signal" Judas gave to the guards who were to apprehend Jesus in the Garden of Gethsemane that fateful night of Holy Thursday? The "holy" kiss. What made it all the more sinister was that Judas used this as a prearranged sign of betrayal of Jesus before the guards.

BEHIND THE SCENES

The first reading tells us that the Lord stood with Moses, and later that "Moses made haste to bow his head toward the earth, and worshipped" (Ex 34:8). The closeness in proximity further echoes this "intimacy" spoken about in the Beyond Words section. God is not distant but draws near to Moses. In the chapter immediately preceding this week's first reading from Exodus (see chapter 33), God actually "covers" Moses with his hand while his glory passes by and overshadows him. Beginning when Moses asked God his holy name (during his encounter with the burning bush), Moses enjoyed an intimacy no one else had known since Adam. While the other patriarchs and leaders who had come before Moses knew God in different ways and had divine and angelic interactions, Moses's interactions were the most physical, tangible, and intimate. During this time, too, in the following chapters of Exodus, God begins to prescribe for Moses how he wants his people to worship him—including the elements and devices we ought to use: altars, vestments, candles, and so on. Sound familiar?

WORD PLAY

Condemnation is normally associated with being found guilty of something or scorn being felt. The word *condemn* comes from the Latin *condemnare*, meaning "to inflict loss upon" someone. When we condemn another, it may mean anything from the loss of a good reputation, to the loss of physical freedom, to prison, or even to the ultimate loss of their life. There is a dramatic irony in the fact that Jesus's underserved condemnation spared us from the condemnation we sinners do deserve. Thank God for his Cross.

JOURNAL

1. How do you view intimacy now after reflecting on the readings and Beyond Words?

2. How does this view differ from the world's view of intimacy?

3. How can you start making your prayer life more intimate?

CHALLENGE FOR THE WEEK

Set aside thirty minutes to go to an adoration chapel near you. When we adore him in this profound prayer, we are drawing into an intimate relationship with him. Look up at Christ with loving eyes and an open heart. Accept his love just as you give love to him.

The Bread of Life

Solemnity of the Most Holy Body and Blood of Christ

OPENING PRAYER

Lord Jesus Christ, thank you for the gift of the Eucharist. Send your Holy Spirit upon me as I read your Word today, so that I might gain a deeper understanding of this beautiful sacrament. The Eucharist is a clear sign of how desperately you desire to be in union with us, so I pray that my heart would be open to you this Sunday more than ever before. Amen.

> **First Reading:** Deuteronomy 8:2–3, 14b–16a
> **Responsorial Psalm:** Psalm 147:12–15, 19–20
> **Second Reading:** 1 Corinthians 10:16–17
> **Gospel:** John 6:51–58

BEYOND WORDS

Have you ever slothfully "wobbled" away from the Thanksgiving dinner table and thought to yourself, "I'm never eating again"? Perhaps you began to wish you'd worn sweatpants as the button on your pants was one exhale away from breaking free and potentially harming nearby relatives. No matter how full you were, though, eventually you ate again. The food, no matter how tasty, only satiated your hunger temporarily.

The Israelites understood hunger and thirst far better than we do. When we pick up this story in Deuteronomy (our first reading), we are being reminded of their wanderings in the desert for forty years, where they survived, daily, on manna and water provided by God. This daily bread may have sustained them physically, but their life depended on this bread and was, thus, very much day by day. This was the backdrop Jesus reminds the people of in the gospel. During this Bread of Life discourse, Christ draws on Israel's history to give them a glimpse at their (and our) future.

The Living Water and Bread of Life was offering them food and drink that will never run dry, never leave them hungry or thirsty again. Christ isn't offering a temporary solution to physical hunger but an eternal solution to spiritual hunger: God's literal and glorified flesh and blood—that is the cup we partake in and the bread we share.

So perfect and filled with love is God that he offers us this gift not once, but repeatedly. The Father calls the family together to his table weekly—daily, in fact—to partake in heaven while still on Earth. Perhaps that is why the Greek word for "thanksgiving" is *eucharistia* because we are sent forth from his table so full that everyone around us is in danger of coming into contact with his great love.

RELATED FACT

The first reading from Deuteronomy reminds us that "man shall not live by bread alone, but by every word that proceeds from the mouth of God" (Dt 8:3). During his duel with the devil in the desert, this is the first thing Jesus says to Satan (see Matthew 4:4). In fact, all three of Jesus's responses are quotes from scripture. After forty days of fasting, when offered food, the Lord drops some timeless truth from the Old Testament before he drops the mic.

BEHIND THE SCENES

Several Old Testament men serve as *prefigurements* of Christ. A prefigurement is an early indication or image of something to come later. Moses is one of the most iconic prefigurements in that Christ's life and mission mirror his in numerous ways.

1. Moses was born and put in a wicker basket. Jesus was born and put in a wooden manger.

2. Moses's life was in danger from a murderous pharaoh. Jesus's life was in danger from the murderous King Herod.

3. Moses turned water into blood (see Exodus 7). Jesus turned water into wine (see John 2).

4. Moses prescribed the Passover lamb to be sacrificed. Jesus became the Passover lamb who was sacrificed.

5. Moses appointed seventy rulers over Israel. Jesus appointed seventy disciples to the nations.

6. Moses and Jesus both fasted alone for forty days, both offered compassion to women beside a well, both gave us the law from atop a mountain, both taught their followers to pray, both were almost stoned by the people, both controlled the sea, and both died on a hill—just to name a few likenesses.

In Moses's example, God began to prepare his people for his own Son, offering Jesus a long and rich tradition and history to point back to in an effort to help the Jews of his time to have a far deeper insight into his identity and his Father's fidelity.

WORD PLAY

The Greek word for *flesh* used by St. John in this famous passage was *sarx*, which means literal, raw human flesh. This word would have undoubtedly caused confusion and, even, disgust for many of those listening (as evidenced by John 6:66). *Sarx* is also the root of the word *sarcasm*, meaning "to tear the flesh of another."

JOURNAL

1. How do you approach Holy Communion? Are you intentionally aware of what's going on during the Mass at this time, or are you spacing out or going through the motions?

2. Do you remember your First Communion? Why did you have a strong desire to receive our Lord sacramentally?

3. What does it mean to you to know that Christ abides in you?

4. Do you view your relationship with Christ as something vital to your survival?

CHALLENGE FOR THE WEEK

If you're struggling to crave the Eucharist, fast for two hours before you go to Mass the next time. You definitely don't have to do this every Sunday, but maybe being intentional about your fasting will help you reflect on the importance of Who you're receiving.

Mercy, Not Sacrifice

Tenth Sunday in Ordinary Time

OPENING PRAYER

Lord, help me to be authentically yours. In all I say, think, and do, may my life be only a reflection of your great mercy and love. Hold me close to you as I desire to grow deeper as your trusted disciple. Amen.

> **First Reading:** Hosea 6:3–6
> **Responsorial Psalm:** Psalm 50:1, 8, 12–13, 14–15
> **Second Reading:** Romans 4:18–25
> **Gospel:** Matthew 9:9–13

BEYOND WORDS

How merciful are you when someone wrongs you? Are you quick to forgive or, even, quicker to judge and condemn? What if your salvation and eternal life were based on how merciful you are and how well you forgive; would that concern you? Yeah, me, too.

In this week's gospel, Jesus is actually quoting the prophet Hosea (this week's first reading) when he says, "I desire mercy, and not sacrifice." (See Hosea 6:6 and Matthew 9:13.) Hosea was preaching and speaking out against the rampant sin that was occurring in the Northern Kingdom of Israel during his time. The nation was filled with idolatry, rebelling against the very God who blessed them with everything they had. By quoting Hosea, Jesus was drawing a parallel between the selfishness of his people in the past and those whom he lived among in his present time. The Pharisees acknowledged Jesus with their lips but denied him in their lifestyle. They "offered sacrifices" to God but cast judgment on their fellow man in a way that was self-righteous and completely lacking in mercy.

While God does call us to sacrifice, it should not be done at the expense of others or in a way that condemns. When we lead with

ORDINARY TIME

121

mercy (as God does), love is revealed. When we lead with condemnation (as the devil does), love is eradicated—and where love is absent, hell pervades.

RELATED FACT

The book of the prophet Hosea describes the unhappy marriage between a man and his wife. The wife is unfaithful to her husband, but he takes her back. The story demonstrates the way in which God always takes back his people even when they are unfaithful to him.

BEHIND THE SCENES

The "customs post" is where taxes were collected. In Galilee, tax collection would have required that Matthew interacted not only with Jews but, also, with Gentiles (who were despised by "good" Jews). Tax collectors were disliked not only for their monetary cheating but, also, for their connection to "unclean" Gentiles. Jesus's calling of Matthew shows not only his dismissal of cultural bias and racism but, also, his desire for all sinners to receive his mercy and to know the Father's love. Calling Matthew—who would undoubtedly have been despised by Jews like Simon (later, Peter), Andrew, James, and John—to join his growing group of disciples also signaled to his closest followers that none were too good or too "bad" to be included in the new kingdom Jesus was ushering in.

WORD PLAY

The word *Pharisee* comes from a Hebrew word that means "separate." Pharisees separated themselves from most of society, which they considered sinful, in an effort to stay clean. At the time of Jesus, they were the popular religious political party (see John 7:48). They came on to the scene about two hundred years before Christ, when the Greeks were forcing the Jews to abandon their religious practices. What began as a good and necessary thing—separation from sinfulness—however, became more of a bad thing over time.

JOURNAL

1. Have you, like the Pharisees, ever deemed another person almost unworthy of God's mercy? What led you to that conclusion?

2. How can you serve those who are on the margins in your community?

3. When volunteering our time to help those in need, it is easy to fall into the trap of thinking we are their "savior." How can you resist this mentality in your life?

CHALLENGE FOR THE WEEK

Pick someone to pray for this week that you wouldn't typically pray for. Whether it be an enemy, a stranger you've judged, or a friend or coworker you struggle to understand, offer your prayers out of a genuine desire for their good.

Reconciled and Righteous

Eleventh Sunday in Ordinary Time

OPENING PRAYER

Lord, thank you for your sacrifice on the Cross. Though I am unworthy of this perfect gift, I accept it with all that I am. May I never take your sacrifice for granted. I ask this through Christ, our Lord. Amen.

First Reading: Exodus 19:2–6a
Responsorial Psalm: Psalm 100:1–2, 3, 5
Second Reading: Romans 5:6–11
Gospel: Matthew 9:36–10:8

BEYOND WORDS

God is active—eternally active. God does not sit and wait; God pursues.

This week we hear not only how Jesus was "filled with pity" but that he does something about it. The Israelites were lost. They were "like sheep without a shepherd," so Christ, "the Lord of the harvest," appoints more laborers to send out. Jesus picks twelve to *go out* and serve in his name.

It would have been easier *not* to pick, train, and empower apostles, but Jesus did. Why? Because God is actively seeking our salvation. God wants all to know his love and mercy. The harvest needs laborers, people who are willing to share the Gospel and the reality of the saving power of his Cross (explored in the second reading). God desired—from the beginning—our holiness. He is the One who pursues and saves us (first reading) in good times and in bad times, throughout our wanderings, both literal and spiritual.

He effectively tells the apostles not to stay but to "go"—to move, to "get out of here," as there is work to be done for the kingdom to come. There are sick to be cured, dead to be raised, lepers to cleanse, and demons to drive out. If they don't do it, who will? By extension, we, as his Church, have the same responsibility and call. God is active always, and that activity is seen in those who know, love, and serve him.

RELATED FACT

Jesus chose his twelve apostles from among dozens of disciples who had begun following him before. *Disciple* means "student," while *apostle* means "one who is sent." In choosing twelve of them, Jesus is mirroring the twelve tribes of Israel that we hear about in the Old Testament.

BEHIND THE SCENES

The twelve apostles are mentioned consistently in the gospels, but many have wondered why some have "two names" or go by different names. In the case of Simon Peter, it's because of the noteworthy moment when Jesus changes his name to signal a change in his essence, vocation, and role as the "rock" and first pope.

In other cases, however, it is because the apostles had two names or in an effort to differentiate apostles who shared the same name. Bartholomew, for instance, is also known as Nathanael (in the Gospel of John), with the former believed to identify his family name and the latter being a more personal designation. Jude (short for Judas) also has two names but goes by Thaddeus as well. The early Church was trying to intentionally show the difference between him and his closely named (yet evil) counterpart, Judas Iscariot. James, the son of Alphaeus, is also known as James "the lesser" to demonstrate that the "other" James (Zebedee), who was one of Jesus's closest followers and friends, was closer to the Lord and shared in a closer intimacy with him.

WORD PLAY

The word *compassion* comes from the Latin *compassio*, meaning "to suffer with." When we are compassionate we not only "feel" for the other; we actually enter into their sorrow and walk alongside of them, taking their pain upon ourselves.

125

JOURNAL

1. Are there relationships in your life that are in need of reconciliation? How can you mend these relationships?

2. Is your relationship with God in need of reconciliation? How can you reconcile your relationship with him?

3. Is your life a reflection of the victory Christ won over death? How so? If not, what needs to change?

CHALLENGE FOR THE WEEK

Honor Christ's sacrifice by making your own personal sacrifice for another this week. Embrace a humble attitude and do not seek anything in return for this sacrificial gift—not even affirmations or accolades.

No Secrets

Twelfth Sunday in Ordinary Time

OPENING PRAYER

Dear Jesus, you have fought for me and continue to do so with the strongest armor. You call me as your own. You desire my whole heart, nothing less. I give myself to you, Lord. Everything I am belongs to you. You are my hope, my strength, and my Savior. Amen.

> **First Reading:** Jeremiah 20:10–13
> **Responsorial Psalm:** Psalm 69:8–10, 14, 17, 33–35
> **Second Reading:** Romans 5:12–15
> **Gospel:** Matthew 10:26–33

BEYOND WORDS

Hide and Seek is—scripturally speaking—the oldest game in creation. We are reminded (in the second reading) that while God was seeking Adam and Eve they were in hiding, seeking their own desires and will. This is how sin entered.

As a result, God went on a rescue mission, saving us from ourselves, even though we—as sinners—don't deserve it. He sent prophets like Jeremiah to unfaithful, unrepentant people, such as his contemporaries who were living in Judah. Even today, God is constantly beckoning and inviting people to turn their hearts back to him, though few take him up on the invitation.

We are reminded in this week's gospel that *everything is exposed* in God's light. Nothing escapes God's glance. He sees all, knows all, and is in all places. No detail, no matter how small, is missed by God. (He even knows the exact number of hairs on your head!) Seeing all of our deeds—even the ones we think we "hide" from him—demonstrates that we are sinners, and not only do we need the mercy of Jesus, but those of us who are too prideful and refuse it will suffer the consequences. We hide because we sin. He seeks because he is

Mercy. Jesus is trying to tell us that eternity is no "game" to God, and we would be wise to trust him more than ourselves.

RELATED FACT

The book of Jeremiah was written sometime between (roughly) AD 630 and 580, and it is filled with prophetic warnings to the Southern Kingdom of Israel, Judah. Judah had been swept up into rampant idolatry after a series of horrible, unvirtuous kings and religious leaders, and was immersed in immorality and pagan worship when God sent the young prophet to warn them, urging them to repent of their sinful, misguided ways.

BEHIND THE SCENES

In the second reading from Paul to the persecuted Christians living in Rome, the great missionary saint and evangelist is trying to explain how original sin "works." God had already warned Adam (and Eve) that death was the consequence of sin. Even knowing this, the original couple chose themselves over the blessing, bringing immediate death of their souls.

This original act of rebellion affected all of us as their descendants. We all bear the mark of Adam and are born with the stain of original sin, a stain that only Baptism can wash away. The separation brought on by our sin is erased by the Sacrament of Baptism, both inviting us and allowing us into the family of God. So "as sin came into the world through one man (Adam) and death through sin," we know that through one person (Jesus), sin was destroyed and the great divide that sin brings was eclipsed through our Lord and Savior, Jesus Christ.

WORD PLAY

The name *Jeremiah* means "the Lord will exalt." Anyone who has read his book or who hears this passage may have a difficult time believing this truth. But, in time, the prophet Jeremiah—often dismissed and disliked by his peers—is proven correct, faithful, and vindicated when God's warnings came to fruition.

JOURNAL

1. How well do you trust God? Would you be willing to give up your most prized possession if he asked you?

2. What in your life have you given to God? How has he taken care of it for you? What in your life right now is God calling you to give to him? Is this difficult for you? Why?

3. Jesus is perpetually fighting for you. How do you fight for him?

CHALLENGE FOR THE WEEK

When we trust in God, we can better accept his mercy. Every day this week, take ten minutes to pray the Divine Mercy Chaplet. This prayer was given to St. Faustina by God to express her trust in his mercy. If you do not know this prayer, you can easily find it online.

Prophets and Losses

Thirteenth Sunday in Ordinary Time

OPENING PRAYER

Almighty God, even after all else fades away, you remain. Help me to make you the constant in my life. Open my heart as I reflect on today's readings so that I might understand the importance of investing in what truly matters. Jesus, I love you. Help me to love you more. Amen.

> **First Reading:** 2 Kings 4:8–11, 14–16a
> **Responsorial Psalm:** Psalm 89:2–3, 16–19
> **Second Reading:** Romans 6:3–4, 8–11
> **Gospel:** Matthew 10:37–42

BEYOND WORDS

How far are you willing to go for God? What limits have you put on following him? Perhaps you will go wherever he calls you to go, or maybe you've drawn a line in the sand with God by telling him you'll do "this and this" but *not* this (like moving or changing jobs). Maybe you'll follow God as long as it doesn't mean you have to be too uncomfortable.

This week's readings remind us that God is more concerned with heaven than Earth, with eternity than the temporary, and with prophets over profits.

Jesus is clear in the gospel: Don't let anything come between you and him. Love God above anything, and everything will work out. Will it be comfortable? No, there will be crosses (and losses) involved, but you will be happy, and you will be saved. St. Paul tells us in the second reading that our Baptism doesn't buy us earthly riches but, rather, opens the door to heavenly glory. If you are with God, you'll be taken care of, as we see with his prophet Elisha in the first reading. Not only that, but countless people will be blessed by your holy

example. The prophets didn't seek a title, nor did they set out for glory; they were merely obedient (unto death), and because of their obedience, they are still revered and God's words (through them) are still read today. God invests in us and sees prophets in the long run.

RELATED FACT

The gospel speaks a lot about "the righteous man." Elsewhere in the Bible a righteous man is compared to a palm tree. That is to say, a righteous man—walking with and connected to God—will grow strong and straight like a palm tree. Just as a palm tree is upright and seems to be soaring to the heavens, so will a Godly person grow quickly and steadily, yearning for and reaching out to the Lord. Just as a palm tree produces good fruit, so will a righteous soul.

BEHIND THE SCENES

St. Paul is the master of saying a great deal in just a few words. All of St. Paul's writings are deep, but his Letter to the Romans is especially so; the letter to Romans is Paul's greatest theological feat and his *magnum opus* (Latin for "great work").

What does it mean that "all of us who have been baptized into Christ Jesus were baptized into his death" (Rom 6:2)? Or that we are buried with him through Baptism?

Here in chapter 6 of Romans, St. Paul is squashing some short-sighted thinking. Some began to think, "Hey, if our sin brings grace, why not just sin even more and let the floodgates of grace open wide?" (see Romans 5:20). Paul is clarifying that the purpose of God's grace is to forgive us of our sins and to help us *not* to sin in the future.

In the midst of this clarification, Paul uses this moment to explain that Baptism unites us to Christ and, given this fact, our sins are put to death because of our union to him and to his Cross. That's why we are "baptized into Jesus's death." We are "buried with him" as we are submerged under the baptismal waters (early Baptisms were full body immersion), but rather than dying under the water we will rise out of it.

The good news about being united to Jesus and being baptized into Christ's death means that we are also united in his victory over death and, through our Baptism, rise to new life! This is why St. Paul so confidently declares that we are dead to sin and "walk in newness of life" (Rom 6:4). Amen!

WORD PLAY

The term *prophet* comes from the Hebrew word for "mouthpiece." Far more than "fortune tellers" or wannabe psychics, the prophets were given a message by God to share with his people and, by God, they did.

JOURNAL

1. What part of your life has God been calling you to surrender to him? Why are you hesitant?

2. Does prayer have a place on your to-do list? How do you think it would affect your day if you made prayer the highest priority?

3. Do you see Christ in other people? What is he trying to reveal about himself to you, through others?

4. How can Christ reveal himself to others through you? What quality do you have that can glorify God?

CHALLENGE FOR THE WEEK

If you say you don't have time for prayer, make time. Every day this week, wake up an hour earlier and start your day right. Take a shower, eat a good breakfast, and spend fifteen or thirty minutes in prayer. Christ will reward your effort!

The Yoke's on You

Fourteenth Sunday in Ordinary Time

OPENING PRAYER

Jesus, you are my everything. It is you—who are humble, caring, forgiving, perfect, strong, faithful, and loving—I admire and strive to be like. Help me to be like you. Give me the grace to match my actions, my thoughts, and my will to yours. Amen.

First Reading: Zechariah 9:9–10
Responsorial Psalm: Psalm 145:1–2, 8–11, 13–14
Second Reading: Romans 8:9, 11–13
Gospel: Matthew 11:25–30

BEYOND WORDS

When you ask professional athletes who they looked up to when they were kids, they inevitably point to the athletes and stars who came before them. You hear them discuss the first time they saw their favorite athlete play the game or how they practiced nonstop until they could throw or shoot like they could. The current stars didn't just "admire" the former all-stars; they sought to be just like them, almost to *become* them. With that in mind, listen to these words from today's gospel. Jesus isn't inviting followers to admire him or to praise him. No, he is inviting disciples (students) to come with him and "become" smaller versions of him.

Knowing that not all who hear the message will follow, Jesus directs his message not to the most learned but, rather, to the most humble. This theme of humility and discipleship is woven throughout the first reading from Zechariah, too. The prophet is not only pointing to the King who would come, humbly mounted upon an ass, but reminding us to rejoice that we have a Savior so meek yet mighty. This would have been a confusing prophecy when it was first uttered but, in God's time, it proved quite powerful. It's important that we

view and embrace the readings through God's divine perspective and not merely our earthly ones. If the spirit is leading the flesh, we see and live as God does, which is what St. Paul is pointing out in the second reading. If we are humble, the Holy Spirit will guide the flesh away from death and toward eternal life.

RELATED FACT

A "yoke" is a harness fit around the neck and shoulders of an animal to tow and guide farming equipment. The animal "saddled" with a yoke was under the instruction of their master for a purpose. Jesus is inviting us to submit to his mastery and guidance, which will lead to our vocation bearing fruit and ultimate joy in the everlasting harvest.

BEHIND THE SCENES

How can the work of bearing this "yoke" leave us feeling restful? How often do you—after a hard day's work or long workout—feel really energized and well-rested?

Seemingly paradoxically, Christ is inviting his disciples into a deeper spiritual reality. If we answer the call to follow Christ and emulate his life, we will not have interior burden, stress, or anxiety. We will have freedom and, through that freedom, peace (and rest) for our souls. This doesn't mean we will never get annoyed or angry but, rather, that those normal human emotions will not upend us because the inner peace we experience will be rooted in a much larger perspective. When we understand that God is always with us, we begin to trust in his presence and blessing even when the day is long and the workload overbearing. Even the yoke upon our shoulders will feel lighter the more we love and trust the One who placed it there.

Jesus is trying to help his followers understand that while discipleship is far from easy, it will not and should not feel like an excessive "burden" either. If we are in line with the will of God and surrender to his perfect plan, we will not feel worn down like slaves but soaring high and free.

WORD PLAY

The word *dominion* comes to us via the Latin *dominus*, meaning "Lord" or "master." In this week's readings, we are being invited to place ourselves beneath the "dominion" or the lordship and gentle mastery of our perfect God.

JOURNAL

1. Who do you look up to? What about this person is admirable?

2. Do any of these qualities resemble qualities of Jesus?

3. In what ways does your spirit lead your flesh?

4. In what ways do you allow your flesh to lead your spirit? What can you do to change this?

CHALLENGE FOR THE WEEK

Take one of the areas in your life where your flesh leads your spirit and work on it. Stay away from this temptation that often takes you over. Really strive to lead with your spirit in this area.

Rich as Dirt

Fifteenth Sunday in Ordinary Time

OPENING PRAYER

Loving Father, thank you for all the blessings you've bestowed upon me today. I pray that you would grant me one more: the grace to understand your teachings and to truly develop a relationship with you. Protect me from the thorns that might try to steal my life from you. Help me to stay rooted in you, my God. Amen.

> **First Reading:** Isaiah 55:10–11
> **Responsorial Psalm:** Psalm 65:10–14
> **Second Reading:** Romans 8:18–23
> **Gospel:** Matthew 13:1–23

BEYOND WORDS

What are the two things (beyond people and pets, obviously) that you would grab from your house if it were on fire? Cell phone? Jewelry? An album of family pictures? Where would your Bible fall on that list? Is it something that is well-used and personal and meaningful? Is it a precious possession, one you want to pass along as an heirloom, or is it an easily replaceable "book"? Would you grab it or not and, if not, what would need to change in your life for it to become all the more precious?

Jesus Christ is the eternal Word of God; scripture is the sacred words about the Word (Jesus). We hear in this first reading from Isaiah that God's Word does his will. He sends it out—gifts it to creation—and it does not "return to [God] empty," meaning when it fulfills his will it bears fruit. In the gospel, Christ compares the Word of God to a seed (which you can read more about below in Behind the Scenes), and what do good seeds do in good soil? They bear fruit. The psalm, too, discusses seeds and fruit and the joy that comes in due time with the harvest.

In the middle of all these agricultural references and parables, we hear St. Paul discussing the sufferings of this world (as fleeting) and the glory of the next (as everlasting), and he compares a sinful life and a life of grace to childbirth, where a couple's love *bears fruit*. When we are open to God, surrendering our lives, hearts, futures (and, yes, even fertility—we are a very pro-life Church) to him, the Word finds rich soil in which to bear fruit, cast away darkness, offer freedom, and bring life. The question is not whether or not God casts seeds but what condition the soil of our heart is in, each day, as he casts. Daily praying of scripture—our most valuable family heirloom—and frequenting the sacraments are the best ways to keep our soil rich.

RELATED FACT

Just as we saw in the beginning of the Sermon on the Mount, we read again in this passage that (Jesus) "sat down" to teach. This gesture and posture clearly denotes Jesus as a rabbi, since sitting was the customary teaching posture of the rabbinical priest toward his disciples, who would sit at his feet.

BEHIND THE SCENES

The parable of the sower and seed is one of the most famous of all Jesus's parables (though the prodigal son usually takes top billing). It's extremely important because understanding this parable sets a foundation of understanding for all the others, while giving the perfect simile by which to judge our own openness and posture as hearers.

The differing soils obviously depict the different postures of heart and responses of people to the Gospel message then and now. Anyone who refuses to listen, is self-consumed, or is easily distracted is depicted in the first situation where the seed falls upon the path, is trampled, and eventually is devoured by birds (which represent evil demons in many commentaries).

Next, we hear about those who hear the Gospel message and excitedly follow, only to quickly die off when any suffering or

persecution comes their way. These are the "feel-good" followers looking for an answer but never a problem. We see this not only in those who welcomed Christ on Palm Sunday yet shouted, "Crucify him!" on Good Friday, but also still today in those who abandon the reality of the crucifix for the lure of a "shinier, softer" cross.

The third soil offers life, but the plant dies from the thorns (the allure of worldly riches and temptations) that choke it, so this soil bears no fruit. We see this in various ways: in our need to control and to "play God," in the ways creation distracts us from our Creator, when we place our trust in man rather than God, and within the contraceptive culture we find ourselves. The final soil—the rich soil—not only stands the test of time and bears fruit, but it bears an abundant harvest by the grace of God. The need to be "rooted" firmly in the faith is evident, as is our need for the Divine Light and Living Water that will raise us up from seeds to producers of fruit.

WORD PLAY

Parables were Jesus's favorite teaching device. From the Latin *parabola* or the Greek *parabolē*, the word means "comparison" and was a popular allegorical method of teaching in the Mediterranean world. Easily remembered and shared by the listeners, the parables frequently shocked and altered the perceptions of the listeners, gave them new insights into the mind and heart of God, and left them with a tangible challenge to be lived out moving forward.

JOURNAL

1. Look back to a time you made a choice that was in line with God's will. Can you think of some fruits that came from that?

2. Are you open to the seeds God is trying to plant within your soil? Or do you feel too busy, satisfied, or angry to grow closer to him?

3. Do you struggle to pay attention during times of prayer? How can you change that?

4. Who is someone that can keep you accountable for keeping the soil of your heart in a good place to receive God's seed?

CHALLENGE FOR THE WEEK

Keep your Bible with you as much as you can this week. Don't take it into the bathroom with you, but keep it in your backpack or purse, or perhaps place it on your desk as you work or on your nightstand as you sleep. Keeping the Bible near you, rather than collecting dust on your bookshelf, will encourage you to read it more. Read and reflect on a few verses, and underline or highlight whatever catches your attention. You'll discover that having scripture so accessible will change the way you pray and approach situations the more you pray with it.

The Good, the Bad, and the Ugly

Sixteenth Sunday in Ordinary Time

OPENING PRAYER

Lord, thank you for the gift of these parables. Through them, may we come to understand how we can allow you to help us grow. Grant us the strength to turn to you in all moments, that we may weed out the evil in our lives and our actions may yield good and bountiful wheat. Amen.

> **First Reading:** Wisdom 12:13, 16–19
> **Responsorial Psalm:** Psalm 86:5–6, 9–10, 15–16
> **Second Reading:** Romans 8:26–27
> **Gospel:** Matthew 13:24–43

BEYOND WORDS

It's been said that nice guys finish last. As a kid did you ever study hard for a test to receive a C, only to see a friend cheat and get the A? Have you ever gotten annoyed because doing what was right was so hard in the moment or really hurt in the long run? Are you ever discouraged by how challenging it can be to live the Christian life when others who reject or don't know God seem to have it so easy or seem to find success through their self-centeredness?

The truth is that this is not a new struggle. This frustration has been going on since the beginning—all the way back to Genesis—when we see the division between people who seek the Lord and those who seek merely the self. This first reading from Wisdom is praising (and imploring) the Lord to continue to be justice to and for all. The passage not only praises God for his mercy but begs him to protect his children from injustice. The psalm, too, praises God for his goodness and mercy, and the second reading from Romans

expresses how powerful the Holy Spirit's (and Jesus's) intercession is for all of us at the feet of the Father.

God is mercy, which is part of the reason that God permits certain evils right now. As Christ teaches us in the Gospel, God is far more patient with us than we are with him. He allows some weeds for a time but not for all time, and there is always hope in Christ that evil hearts will open and turn to the good. In his patience and mercy, Christ gives us every opportunity to turn our hearts fully toward him. When the time's up, though, there will be a division and a casting out. Justice will come in a way many are not expecting. In the end, nice guys do finish first; it's just a matter of remembering that the goal is heaven, not earth.

RELATED FACT

The mustard seed is botanically (and parabolically) known as the smallest of all seeds, yet it can grow to be a large, substantial bush (almost a tree). Jesus gives those of us not familiar with mustard plants or agriculture a glimpse into the size of the mustard seed, informing us that the bush grows large enough to hold and house many birds, in fact.

BEHIND THE SCENES

Note that within the gospel story Jesus changes locations and audiences. A seemingly "minor" detail that is actually quite important appears in verse 36, which reads, "Then he left the crowds and went into the house. And his disciples came to him."

This change in location offers the Lord more time for private instruction of his disciples, away from the growing crowds. It is only after this change in location (a detail inspired by the Holy Spirit through the pen of St. Matthew) that we see Jesus actually explain and unpack the deeper meaning of the parable in regard to God's mercy and the final judgment. Note that even though the farmer (God) allows the weeds and wheat to coexist, a time will come when they will be separated. The separation will be easy because you'll be

able to see which produce fruit and which do not (as seen through our actions and good deeds on Earth).

The parable demonstrates that in God there is patience, yes, but in God there is also ultimate justice. The faithful followers of the Lord will be vindicated and glorified, while those who have led the Lord's children into sin will be punished and face the worst possible consequences.

WORD PLAY

The "weeds" mentioned here are most likely called *darnel*, known in the plant kingdom as *Lolium temulentum*. The darnel is a poisonous plant that gets intertwined with wheat and gets increasingly attached to it as the wheat approaches harvest. If removed prematurely, the darnel would absolutely take with it viable and valuable wheat.

JOURNAL

1. What is the most difficult part about being a Christian?

2. Why is it so challenging to live as a true Christian in the twenty-first century, specifically?

3. What is one way you have had to grow in the past year to become a better person? Was it worth it? Why?

4. What is one way you need to grow this coming month to become holier?

CHALLENGE FOR THE WEEK

Take ten minutes to write out a specific prayer asking God to help you grow this next month to become a better person. Pray this prayer every day for the next few weeks.

An Understanding Heart

Seventeenth Sunday in Ordinary Time

OPENING PRAYER

Almighty God, give me the eyes to see situations as you see them, so that I might act as you hope for me to act. Help me to be your hands and feet on Earth, acting in a way that leads others closer to you. When I am tempted to be selfish, rude, or proud, send your Spirit to inspire me to choose love. Amen.

First Reading: 1 Kings 3:5, 7–12
Responsorial Psalm: Psalm 119:57, 72, 76–77, 127–30
Second Reading: Romans 8:28–30
Gospel: Matthew 13:44–52

BEYOND WORDS

While both are important, especially for a leader, wisdom and knowledge are often confused. Both wisdom and knowledge are gifts of the Holy Spirit, and though they work in tandem, they are quite different. Wisdom is the first and highest gift of the Spirit, offering us perspective, right judgment, and detachment from the earthly as we pursue the heavenly. Knowledge gives us the ability and the information to judge truths, but wisdom gives us the desire to judge truth through a more heavenly and divine perspective.

In the first reading we see that King Solomon is said to be "the wisest man who ever walked the planet" because God, himself, says so. When given the opportunity to ask God for anything, Solomon doesn't treat God like a genie, asking for fame or fortune or "more wishes" but, rather, asks for wisdom so that he can govern the people well. Would you do that? St. Paul reminds us in the second reading that *all things work for good* even though we may not readily see it that way. In other words, even the suffering that God allows will ultimately work for our good and help lead us to heaven. The question

143

is what we do with the truth and knowledge we encounter. Do we pursue it immediately and with abandon like the guy who finds buried treasure or the valuable pearl (in this week's gospel), or not? Wisdom dictates that when we encounter God—who is the greatest good—we abandon all for him. God is patient with us, though, and gives us time. Just as we must wisely discern right from wrong and truth from lies, so will God (and his angels) discern and separate the good from the bad in the end, like a fisherman sorting fish.

RELATED FACT

Words matter. There are several words that signal us back to the Holy Spirit that we use in common language. For instance, many in high school or college are familiar with the title *sophomore* and think it preferable to the lowly designation of *freshman*. What many don't know, however, is that *sophomore* actually means "wise fool" (in Greek, *sophia* means "wisdom," and *moron* means "fool").

BEHIND THE SCENES

In this gospel passage, Jesus uses a powerful visual example for anyone with even rudimentary knowledge of the fishing industry. The net our Lord is referring to is a *seine* net, which is typically held between two boats, is dragged, and then is thrown into the sea (this is where the term *dragnet* originates from). The net gathers every type of fish—those edible and valuable and those that are not so. The fishermen take these great nets ashore, where they sort the fish into good and bad piles or buckets.

Jesus employs and juxtaposes this analogy amid his parable of the weeds and the wheat, drawing a powerful parallel that is timeless in its importance. Good and evil coexist in this world. If God comes too soon in judgment, some souls who just needed more time to hear the Gospel message and convert would assuredly be lost and tossed out into the fire (hell). No, the fisherman and farmer here are shown as patient, gathering the bad and the good fish and wheat until the appointed time comes to sort the two. This would have been a very

simple yet quite poignant scene that would no doubt be called to mind by Jesus's listeners at the close of each fishing day and every farming season.

WORD PLAY

The word *discern* is popular in Church circles as a way of talking about prayerfully figuring out what God wants from us and for us, especially as it pertains to our vocation. Discernment comes from the Latin *discernere*, which means "to separate apart" (*dis* means "apart," and *cernere* means "to separate"). Quite literally, when we discern, we separate different facets to the question or decision that lie before us, removing our own emotions, opinions, and desires from the equation to, first, get a better understanding of God's will for us.

JOURNAL

1. The man in today's gospel sells all that he has out of joy. Do you allow yourself to feel the joy of loving and being loved by Christ? Or do you keep your distance from him?

2. Do you view the Lord's commands as helpful guidance? Or are they rules contrary to your natural inclination? How can you fix that?

3. Do you take time to consider how God wants you to respond to a situation, or do you react quickly? What happens as a result?

4. Do you try to make decisions on your own, or do you consult someone wise first? Why?

CHALLENGE FOR THE WEEK

This week, fast from an earthly item you really enjoy, such as coffee or soda, listening to music in the car, or that drink after dinner. Every time you would normally go to it, pray for the gift of wisdom and right judgment instead. As much as you like this earthly item, spending a week without it will show you that it really doesn't matter to you that much. Your true treasure lies in heaven.

Love Conquers All

Eighteenth Sunday in Ordinary Time

OPENING PRAYER

Thank you, Lord, for the many ways you provide for me. Thank you for the big gifts and the very little ones, for the complex ones and the simple ones. May I remember these good and perfect gifts today as I go about my day. Amen.

> **First Reading:** Isaiah 55:1–3
> **Responsorial Psalm:** Psalm 145:8–9, 15–16, 17–18
> **Second Reading:** Romans 8:35, 37–39
> **Gospel:** Matthew 14:13–21

BEYOND WORDS

We are all consuming something. Whether it is what we take in visually through social media, video, or our conversations, or what we literally consume through eating, what we "consume" has an effect on us. Just the way the food we eat impacts us physically, what we take into our minds can have an effect on us emotionally, mentally, and spiritually.

Unfortunately, we rarely stop to really consider what we consume and how it impacts us. Our lives are busy and we move quickly, absorbing hundreds of thousands of sounds, images, videos, interactions, conversations, and messages daily. On top of that, we "consume" materials in what we buy and desire. Despite all this consumption, it is easy to feel empty. We consume but are not satisfied.

The prophet Isaiah proclaims a hopeful message from God in the first reading. In it, God promises that he is going to provide for what people need—what they really need—and it isn't going to cost them anything. Within the lines is a challenge, "Why do you spend your money for which is not bread, and your labor for that which does not satisfy?" (Is 55:2). We often spend our time, money, and attention on things that fail to satisfy and not what we actually need. We miss the

"bread" that is necessary for us to thrive and chase something else. Isaiah reminds the people that God alone can satisfy.

In a world that is so materially focused, it can be difficult to really pray the psalm this Sunday and mean it: "Thou satisfiest the desire of every living thing" (Ps 145:16). In seeking to be fulfilled, we mistakenly believe that we need to fend for ourselves, but God has more than we could ever ask for. As St. Paul reminds us in his Letter to the Romans, God's gift is given out of love, a love that we cannot be separated from.

This idea of God's providence plays out in dramatic fashion in the gospel. The miraculous feeding of five thousand is one of the only miracle stories (in addition to the Resurrection) that appears in all four gospels, and all four include the same line, "They all ate and were satisfied." This miracle story is a direct fulfillment of the prophecy from Isaiah. Jesus provides for people, without cost, and they find what they are looking for. We experience this same providence in the Eucharist, the true bread that gives us all we need. When we consume it, we become like Christ, and Christ resides in us. We are all consuming something, but there is only one thing that we will ever consume that can not only satisfy us but also save us—Christ himself.

RELATED FACT
Each American consumes, on average, fifty-three pounds of bread per year.

BEHIND THE SCENES
The miraculous feeding of five thousand is a gospel narrative that has been debated by theologians for centuries. Some have proposed that the story is not a miracle of abundance or multiplication of the five loaves and two fish that Jesus was given, but a story of people being so moved by Jesus's action that they go bring food they have to share. While this also could send a good message, the idea that the gospel account is actually a story of sharing and not of God miraculously feeding a multitude misses the mark. Just as we read other miracle stories as being true (and not metaphor), the tradition

of the Church holds that this miracle story is also to be read literally and not figuratively. By an act of God, more food was produced than there originally was (and everyone stayed put as it was passed out).

The miracle is a foreshadowing of the Eucharist, and St. Matthew ties the two together through the same blessing movements. Jesus first takes the loaves and fish, then says a blessing, breaks the loaves, and gives them to the disciples. When you read the narrative of the Last Supper later on in the Gospel of Matthew, the same movements are present as Jesus gives the disciples the Eucharist (see Matthew 26:26).

The message is clear—it is through the Eucharist that we find true satisfaction and that all people, as prophesized by Isaiah, can come and receive without cost the greatest gift and spiritual food and, through it, eternal life.

WORD PLAY

Principalities are an order of angels that are referenced in St. Paul's Letter to the Romans, one of the nine hierarchies of angels.

JOURNAL

1. Have you ever doubted God's love for you? What caused you to question his love? What reminded you of his love?

2. How have you experienced God's love in your life? How has God shown you that he loves you and is always with you?

3. How can your actions toward the people you meet on a daily basis better reflect God's love for you and all people?

CHALLENGE FOR THE WEEK

Keep a journal this week (written down or on your phone). Each day, list one tangible moment in which you experienced God's love. Remember, God loves each of us uniquely. It may be in the colors of the sunrise, or in a song, or in the way your spouse or child or friend says, "I love you," that God speaks. Whatever it is, be consistent and strive to recognize the unique way he exemplifies his love to you daily.

In God's Time

Feast of the Transfiguration of the Lord

OPENING PRAYER

Almighty God, often in life you ask us to wait for good things to come. Sometimes it is hard to accept this. Please teach me, today and always, to be patient and to find peace in each and every moment. I ask that you allow me to see the many incredible ways you are working in my life, even if they are small and hard to see sometimes. Amen.

> **First Reading:** Daniel 7:9–10, 13–14
> **Responsorial Psalm:** Psalm 97:1–2, 5–6, 9
> **Second Reading:** 2 Peter 1:16–19
> **Gospel:** Matthew 17:1–9

BEYOND WORDS

God is timeless; we are not. This simple premise is vital to remember when looking at scripture or at our lives, in general. All things are present to God who exists outside of space and time. Often, we get frustrated or experience fear and anxiety when we try to put God on our timetable, but we can't put the Timeless One "on the clock." In the midst of our sufferings or trials, for instance, our humanity wants a divine solution and antidote immediately, but if God worked on our watch, he wouldn't be God—we would.

In this week's readings, we see the apostles given a great gift and "glimpse" of what is to come, when they behold Christ in his glory. It was like the Lord pulled back the curtain and allowed his closest followers into the throne room of heaven to give them a foreshadowing of what awaits us. God did this, in part, to strengthen these three apostles after the prediction of his impending suffering and death. How often, in the midst of your own stress or fear, do you call out to God asking for some kind of assurance that it is all going to

be okay and work out? Knowing the pain that was to come, the Lord mercifully gave them a vision of what is eternal to remember during the pains to come that would be temporary. Notice the power and stature that the throne and words like *dominion* and *kingship* evoke in the first reading from Daniel. That book was written about a time of great persecution and enslavement of God's children, yet we hear the victorious language. St. Peter's letter, too, was penned as a boost for Christians who were undergoing torturous threats, violence, and martyrdoms under Roman rule.

This Sunday and its readings ought to offer us all hope that no matter how bad the struggle is, nor how intense the suffering gets, those who know the Lord will emerge victorious in due *time*—which is God's time.

RELATED FACT

The gospels never explicitly say that Mount Tabor was the sight of this famous Transfiguration. Oral tradition places the miraculous scene upon Tabor, but not written tradition. Mount Tabor is located about five miles east of Nazareth and roughly eleven miles west of the Sea of Galilee.

BEHIND THE SCENES

If viewed "side by side," you will see several similarities between Moses's encounter with God upon Mount Sinai in Exodus and the apostles' experience of Christ upon Mount Tabor in the gospels. St. Matthew tells us that this event takes place "on the seventh day," just as we see within the Moses account in Exodus 24:16. Both stories (obviously) occur on a mountain, and both result in their faces radiantly shining with God's glory. In Exodus, Moses brings three companions along (Aaron, Nadab, and Abihu); in the gospel, Jesus invites only Peter, James, and John atop the mountain. Finally, both events offer us a glimpse of God's "cloud of glory" as well as an audible experience of the voice of God.

As we see numerous times elsewhere in the Old Testament, the Moses event *prefigures* (foreshadows and prepares) the Transfiguration event of the New Testament. While the similarities and consistencies between the stories may not be easily or readily noticed by most of us "modern" followers of the Lord, they would have been quite obvious to the God-fearing Jews of Jesus's time.

WORD PLAY

Oftentimes in scripture we see that a person's name has more to do with their personality or essence or origin than merely a term of identification. *Adam* (as we've already read) meant "Earth/ground," which pointed to his origin. Simon's name was changed to *Peter*, meaning "rock." *Moses* actually comes from the Hebrew name *Moshee*, which means "out of the water," since the baby prophet was literally fished out of the Nile River by the pharaoh's daughter in Exodus chapter 1. *Elijah* means "the Lord is my God (YHWH)." Moses and Elijah represent the Law and the prophets, the perfect summation of the old covenant meeting the new atop the mountain.

JOURNAL

1. In the presence of the Lord, Peter says, "Lord, it is well that we are here." Have you ever had this same thought in Mass or Eucharistic Adoration? Why or why not?

2. Have you ever experienced God speak clearly to you in a time of great sadness or distress? What did he say?

3. How might the Lord be speaking to you personally through this gospel reading today? How can this great news of Christ's Transfiguration be a beacon of light in your own life?

CHALLENGE FOR THE WEEK

This week, when you kneel to pray before Sunday Mass, praise the Lord and tell him, "It is good that I am here; thank you for inviting me to this feast," and keep this prayer of gratitude in mind throughout the entire Mass.

Walking with God

Nineteenth Sunday in Ordinary Time

OPENING PRAYER

Savior, I ask you today for greater faith. May I be as bold as St. Peter to follow you into the deep, trusting that you will make sure I am always protected. Amen.

> **First Reading:** 1 Kings 19:9a, 11–13a
> **Responsorial Psalm:** Psalm 85:9, 10, 11–12, 13–14
> **Second Reading:** Romans 9:1–5
> **Gospel:** Matthew 14:22–33

BEYOND WORDS

This story of the storm at sea is one of the most famous in all the gospels. In this account, we see the Lord send his apostles straight into a storm while he departs to the safety and serenity of dry land for night prayer. Consider that fact, for a moment. Jesus sent them *into a storm.* Why? Had they gotten on his nerves with their inability to catch fish or their constant questions about who was the best disciple? No. Christ obviously knew what he was doing, allowing his closest followers to go through a storm—and he still does.

Elijah was running for his life and hiding in a cave when God comes and speaks to him (first reading), not in some grandiose gesture of winds or fire, but in a subtle whisper. Are you quiet enough to hear the whisperings of God? Are your eyes open to see his movement around you, or are they too glued to a screen most days? Do you want salvation for your loved ones as badly as St. Paul wants it for the early Christians (second reading)?

Whether or not you are prayerfully seeking God, the good news is that he is seeking you. He's coming into your places of darkness and hiding to speak to you. He's coming out into your storm to save you. Why? Like St. Paul, God wants your salvation even more than

you do. Will you have the humility to extend a hand to heaven at Mass this week and ask the Lord to come and save you once again?

RELATED FACT

The Sea of Galilee is roughly thirteen miles long and approximately six miles wide, but no deeper than 150 feet. The winds that come through the surrounding hill country can quickly kick up a severe storm on and around the water—hence, some of the most dramatic scenes in the gospels.

BEHIND THE SCENES

Scripture stories often do not mean "as much" to us as they ought to because when we read them (or hear them proclaimed at Mass), we are lacking the proper background or context of the story. The first reading from 1 Kings is a prime example of this problem.

This week's reading opens with the prophet Elijah coming forth from the mouth of the cave (a pretty random place to be hanging out, to be sure). We hear that the famous prophet witnesses a mighty wind, an earthquake, and eruptions of fire, but only encounters and "hears" God in the gentle whisper. What we don't hear proclaimed, however, is the location of this cave, what prompted Elijah to be there, and why he was needing direction from the Lord so badly.

In the chapters that precede this well-known scene, though, we are given a glimpse into the mental and physical state of Elijah when the Lord comes. He has just done battle with more than eight hundred false prophets on Mount Carmel. Queen Jezebel wants Elijah dead and is having him hunted down. The prophet Elijah is on the run, praying for death, and has just traveled forty days without food or water into the desert wilderness until he comes to Mount Horeb (also known as Mount Sinai). It's from a cave, upon this famous mountain, that the prophet has this divine and intimate encounter with God, reassuring Elijah of his enduring presence, his promise, and a bright future ahead. We often seek God in the "big ways" and usually when we are at the end of our rope, much like Elijah. If you're

ORDINARY TIME

feeling alone, abandoned, and hopeless as if you've been "walking with the Lord" forever with very little response, keep walking. The Lord is coming for you and probably in ways you are not expecting.

This is the Word of the Lord.

This is why at Mass we reply, "Thanks be to God."

WORD PLAY

The *fourth watch* mentioned in the gospel was a designation of time used by the Romans, who broke their "watches" for guard duty into three-hour shifts. The fourth watch was the dead of night including the final hours of darkness before daybreak, specifically 3:00–6:00 a.m.

JOURNAL

1. Have you ever experienced a moment in which you knew the Lord was present through either an answered prayer or a moment of peace? Explain.

2. Although Peter asks the Lord to call him out upon the water, he still freezes in a moment of fear. Have you ever had that same experience? What helped you get through that fear?

3. Jesus asks Peter why he doubted. What is one area of your life or about the Church that you doubt? What do you think it is that causes you to doubt?

CHALLENGE FOR THE WEEK

Take some time to have a conversation with a trusted friend about this area of doubt in your life. If it is an area of doubt about the Church, seek out a trusted *and knowledgeable* friend in terms of theology. Ask him or her to pray for you or with you, and ask the Lord to strengthen your trust in him.

Fruit of the Womb

Solemnity of the Assumption of the Blessed Virgin Mary

OPENING PRAYER

Pray the Hail Mary (or another of your favorite Marian prayers) to invoke Our Lady's intercession as you begin.

> **(Mass during the Day)**
> **First Reading:** Revelation 11:19a; 12:1–6a, 10ab
> **Responsorial Psalm:** Psalm 45
> **Second Reading:** 1 Corinthians 15:20–27
> **Gospel:** Luke 1:39–56

BEYOND WORDS

"It ain't over until it's over." The famous cliché has been recited countless times in sporting events, elections, and even in movie theaters. There are many variations of the saying, but they all convey the same thing: until the event is done, anything can happen.

The Solemnity of the Assumption of the Blessed Virgin Mary at first can seem like a strange holy day, especially since the readings don't reference Mary's assumption into heaven at all. Instead, they paint a picture of what the end looks like and how we live as we wait for it. Mary's bodily assumption into heaven is a foreshadowing of what will happen to all of us at the end of human history—Jesus returns for the Church, and those who are invited into heaven receive their body back in a glorified way. Along the way, though, the path is a battle.

The first reading paints a fantastic vision of what this battle looks like. St. John, the writer of the book of Revelation, sees the ark of the covenant—a sign of God's abiding presence—in the sky and then a woman, a dragon, and the conflict between the two. In the vision, the dragon seems to be winning and is set to eat the child the woman is giving birth to, but "it ain't over until it's over," and the woman

escapes. The message may be wrapped in apocalyptic imagery, but the message is clear: Evil doesn't win and can't prevail. God always wins. This message can be easy for us to forget or even doubt in a world filled with so much hatred, violence, and suffering.

The early Christians struggled with this reality, as well. Many of them mistakenly believed that Jesus's Second Coming was going to happen shortly after his Resurrection, but when days turned into months and years, they started to worry. St. Paul is writing to the community in Corinth to dispel the misconception that Jesus's lack of a return meant that something had gone wrong. The war was won, but the battle wasn't over.

We live in a time where those words are true for us. We live in a battle, but the war is over. Jesus is victorious, and we can hope in the life Jesus promises us when our lives are over. What do we do in the meantime? We reflect on the gospel and Mary's disposition. Mary visits Elizabeth with a lot of uncertainty in her life. She is newly pregnant with Jesus and perhaps unsure of what that will mean. Instead of focusing on the stress, she chooses joy. She rejoices with Elizabeth, and the two celebrate the incredible things God is doing in their lives. They celebrate God's victory.

God wins, and if it seems as if things are falling apart, remember that "it ain't over until it's over." Rejoice in that victory.

RELATED FACT

Dragons are mentioned in several books of sacred scripture as a representation of danger, evil, or death. Unrelated, Komodo dragons—the largest lizard on Earth—can eat up to 80 percent of their body weight in one meal.

BEHIND THE SCENES

The book of Revelation has long captivated the imagination of Christians, especially in the modern age. It contains a vision given to St. John while he was in exile on an island called Patmos, and the imagery correlates to much of what the early Christian Church was facing,

but also points forward to the ultimate triumph of Christ at the end of time.

The book's imagery can be alarming, so much so that early Christians debated as to whether or not the book should be included in the canon of sacred scripture. Ultimately, it was discerned that the book was inspired by the Holy Spirit and important for Christians of all ages—not just the first-century audience—to remind them that Jesus Christ would one day return and "put all things in subjection under his feet" (1 Cor 15:27).

Many people try to "decode" the book to find particular images or pieces of the vision that correspond to current world events, even going so far as to try to predict the exact date of Jesus's Second Coming. St. John didn't write the book of Revelation for a specific time (other than perhaps the time he was living in). It is important to remember when reading that, for a first-century audience, the vision held a very specific meaning, but for us we should avoid trying to attach current political figures, situations, or places to the vision itself. Instead, we should read the book with a great sense of hope in Jesus's return and confidence in the reality that evil can never win.

WORD PLAY

The book of Revelation is also called the "Apocalypse of St. John." The word *apocalypse* has been associated with the end of the world, but only since the twelfth century. In early Jewish and Christian writing, the word meant "unveiling" and was a writing style that often involved images and symbols to convey a deeper message.

JOURNAL

1. Is there a place or situation where you are "waiting" on God? How can you be joyful in this moment of waiting?

2. Read through the gospel, specifically the prayer of Mary. What words or phrases stand out to you? Why?

3. Who do you know that is experiencing a great blessing in their life right now? Write down their names and a prayer of thanksgiving for each one of them.

CHALLENGE FOR THE WEEK

Who in your life do you need to rejoice with this week? Go find some time to celebrate with them by taking them out to dinner, getting coffee, or simply sending a card congratulating them. Take the time to let them know you are excited for what is happening in their world.

Culture Clash
Twentieth Sunday in Ordinary Time

OPENING PRAYER

Lord God, thank you for the reminder that your Church is a universal one. May I be open, today and always, to learn from everyone around me, even those with a different language and culture. Amen.

> **First Reading:** Isaiah 56:1, 6–7
> **Responsorial Psalm:** Psalm 67:2–3, 5–6, 8
> **Second Reading:** Romans 11:13–15, 29–32
> **Gospel:** Matthew 15:21–28

BEYOND WORDS

Did God come only to save Catholics? No. Did our Lord die on the Cross only to save Christians? Certainly not. Our Lord is the Lord of all!

It's difficult for our modern minds to appreciate the hatred that Jews and Gentiles shared for one another. In this gospel passage, again, we see Jesus (a Jew) interacting with a Gentile (a non-Jew). At first, the dialogue even seems rude (but you can read more about that in the Behind the Scenes section). A closer examination, though, reveals that the Lord is proclaiming that his salvation and his kingdom are open to all—including Gentiles. This was not just good news but fulfilled prophecy. The first reading from Isaiah discusses the "foreigners" (non-Jews) who would "join themselves to the Lord," loving him, serving him, and so on. God foretold that his Temple would be for all peoples.

St. Paul is striking this nerve a little bit in the second reading because he is Jewish, yet explaining, "I am the apostle to the Gentiles, I magnify my ministry in order to make my fellow Jews jealous, and thus save some of them" (Rom 11:14). In this passage, he's talking about the tension in Jews when Gentiles are welcomed into the Body

ORDINARY TIME

159

of Christ, but he's also warning them not to become prideful and potentially "lose" their salvation. These readings are a celebration of the mercy of God, inviting us sinners—of all backgrounds and denominations—to know him more intimately, especially in his holy temple. The gospel demonstrates the power of persistent prayer and the need for faith and humility on our parts. It's not about what faith we were born into, necessarily, but the way we seek the Lord. Talk is cheap; actions speak far louder. It's time we do what is right and just, serve the Lord, and trust in his mercy.

RELATED FACT

Dogs are only mentioned five times in the gospels and never in the Gospel of John. Cats (felines) are not mentioned at all in the gospels . . . just saying.

BEHIND THE SCENES

Tyre and Sidon are cities on the northern coast of the Mediterranean. Because they were filled with Gentiles, Jesus had not yet been to these cities as part of his ministry, but they had obviously already heard of this Jewish wonder-worker from Nazareth. Interestingly in the story, even after the mother has called out to Jesus repeatedly, he does not initially respond to her, stating that he was coming for "the lost sheep of the house of Israel" (meaning the Jews). Israel was known as the "firstborn son" and, as we see throughout the Old Testament, the firstborn is the first one who receives the father's blessings.

Likening the woman and her people to dogs (rather than children) seems a bit "rough" (pun intended), but Jesus isn't being rude. Dogs, then and now, live with a family and are beloved but don't share the same benefits as children do within a household (at least not in a normal, sane household). The woman's humility and submission to God's will and to Jesus as Lord shines through and, in the end, her persistence pays off. The Canaanite woman is praised for her faith and has become a prime gospel model of the power of petitionary prayer.

WORD PLAY

Profanation comes from the Latin term *profanum*, meaning "outside/ in front of the temple" (*pro* means "before or outside," and *fanum* is the root for "temple"). Basically, profanity has no place within the temple, be it the physical place of worship or our bodies, the temples of the Holy Spirit.

JOURNAL

1. Have you ever met someone of a radically different faith or culture? What similarities and differences immediately jumped out at you, if any?

2. Why do you think we so often allow ourselves to look more quickly at our differences than our similarities?

3. Have you ever experienced a time when it was harder to accept God's mercy for yourself than it was for others? Why?

CHALLENGE FOR THE WEEK

Do you know someone well who comes from a different faith background or belief system? Perhaps it's a neighbor or coworker. This week, ask them to tell you more about their church or faith and what they believe. Not for the sake of argument, or for proving you are right, but for the sake of understanding them a little bit better.

The Key Chain

Twenty-First Sunday in Ordinary Time

OPENING PRAYER

Lord God, King of Heaven and Earth, thank you for the gift of St. Peter. Thank you for giving us such a humble and honest leader to guide the Church, your holy bride, to your heavenly banquet. Teach me, today, to honor the authority you left to the popes. May I offer my prayers much faster than I offer my criticism. Amen.

> **First Reading:** Isaiah 22:19–23
> **Responsorial Psalm:** Psalm 138:1–2, 2–3, 6–8
> **Second Reading:** Romans 11:33–36
> **Gospel:** Matthew 16:13–20

BEYOND WORDS

As Catholics, we know well the story of Jesus giving Simon "the keys" to the Church, changing his name to Peter and promising that hell would never vanquish us. What few people know, however, is something revealed to us in the first reading this week from Isaiah. This practice of giving the keys to the prime minister has its roots in the Old Testament. Here we see Eliakim, the prime minister, being given a robe and sash along with a key to demonstrate his authority. He controls the lock, which keeps both intruders out and inhabitants safely in. Note, too, that earlier in the passage we hear that, although Eliakim is a leader, God says, "I will call *my servant*."

St. Paul is so overwhelmed by God's creativity and promise to save the world through Christ, he has to write about it—which he does in this second reading. The psalmist, too, praises God for his mercy, fidelity, and kindness. What we see in the institution of Peter as our first pope is a plan that God had in the making centuries and centuries before. We see God acknowledging our need for a servant leader to bring order to the earthly chaos, to govern us with a heart for God, and to provide his Church—his kingdom on Earth—a firm foundation of truth and mercy upon which to be built. Those keys have been passed through an unbroken chain—a key chain—century after century, ensuring that all have a chance to come to experience God's mercy through his Church here on Earth.

RELATED FACT

The robe and sash (or "girdle" in Hebrew) described in the first reading are signs not only of authority but of a high office. The robe is priestly in nature and the sash or girdle is like a "badge" worn only by military officials, royalty, or someone serving in the priestly office.

BEHIND THE SCENES

Caesarea Philippi was a town in northern Palestine near Mount Hermon. What made the town unique was that Philip, the son of King Herod the Great, built it atop a massive wall of rock estimated to be about one hundred feet high and five hundred feet wide. The city was home to a temple dedicated to Pan, the (false) god of hunting and nature.

Sitting about twenty-five miles from the Sea of Galilee, Caesarea Philippi would have been at least a full day's walk for Jesus and his apostles. Why would Jesus make his closest followers walk that far for a simple teaching? Consider the backdrop. There is no better place in Palestine for Jesus to use as a visual example regarding Simon Peter's new role. Just as Caesarea Philippi was built upon a huge face of rock, so would the kingdom of heaven be built upon "the Rock" now called Peter.

WORD PLAY

The name *Simon* means "listener" or "hearer" in Hebrew. The name change to Peter demonstrates both God's authority and a change in Simon's essence and mission. The name *Peter* means "rock" from the Greek *Petros* or Aramaic *Cephas*.

JOURNAL

1. Jesus asks Simon Peter, "Who do you say that I am?" If Jesus were to ask you that same question today, what would be your response? Who is Jesus in your day-to-day life?

2. Jesus says, "Whatever you bind on earth shall be bound in heaven." What does he mean by this, and how does it correlate to the priesthood and the Sacrament of Reconciliation?

3. How can the Church and her authority guide you to heaven? What kind of attitude does this require on your behalf?

CHALLENGE FOR THE WEEK

We can trace every priest, bishop, cardinal, and pope back to St. Peter through something called apostolic succession. Your parish priest was ordained by a bishop who was ordained by another bishop and so on and so forth, all the way back to this reading when Jesus appointed St. Peter.

Do you know your parish priest? Whether you love him, like him, or "tolerate" him, the fact is that he has been appointed by the bishop to lead his parish flock (including you) to heaven. This week approach your parish priest after Mass, introduce yourself (or say hello if you know him already), and ask how you can pray for him this coming week.

Seriously, God?

Twenty-Second Sunday in Ordinary Time

OPENING PRAYER

Lord, sometimes my suffering feels like too much, and I don't understand why I have to experience this pain. But I recognize that although I may not understand why I experience this suffering, you desire me to do something positive with it. Thank you for giving me knowledge of my suffering so that I can offer it back to you. Amen.

> **First Reading:** Jeremiah 20:7–9
> **Responsorial Psalm:** Psalm 63:2–6, 8–9
> **Second Reading:** Romans 12:1–2
> **Gospel:** Matthew 16:21–27

BEYOND WORDS

If you were offered either "the easy path" or "the hard path," which would you choose? Obviously most everyone would choose the easy path. Life is challenging enough without making it even more difficult for ourselves, right? Who wants to add additional work, strain, and stress to their life? Have you ever had one of those weeks where everything goes wrong and you look up to heaven as if to say, "Seriously, God?"

As we hear this week's readings, though, it doesn't sound like the easy way is God's way. Take Jeremiah, for instance, in this first reading. The young prophet is annoyed—even angry—with God here. Jeremiah realizes that living for God and speaking for him has brought personal hardship and difficulty, yet he knows that God makes it all worth it in the end. St. Paul, likewise, is telling the believers in Rome (under Roman rule) that they should "present [their] bodies as a living sacrifice." He is calling for a physical submission that will bring spiritual freedom and eternal joy. St. Peter is just giving us a natural human response to the news of Jesus's impending suffering in the

ORDINARY TIME

165

gospel passage. Who among us would "wish" any type of suffering upon another, especially the one you care about the most? Jesus is quick to point out, however, that we must not view suffering as the world does. Suffering is a way in which we are challenged and refined in order to grow in holiness and in love. St. Peter didn't understand it that day but, in time, he assuredly did, offering his own body on a cross decades after the Passion, Death, Resurrection, and Ascension. Peter beheld the glory that comes from suffering and testified to it with his own blood.

In Christ and in the Cross, our own sufferings make sense. When times get tough, we need to get going—to Jesus, and keep going with him.

RELATED FACT

In this week's gospel from St. Matthew, we hear the phrase "take up his cross and follow me." Interestingly, in St. Luke's gospel the line adds the word "daily" as in "take up [your] cross *daily* and follow me" (Lk 9:23).

BEHIND THE SCENES

The gospel this week quickly drops several key names and terms such as "elders, the chief priests and the scribes." So, who and what are these people, and how do they relate to the Pharisees and Sadducees?

Elders

The elders were typically older (or "elder") men of stature who were local government leaders, judges, and other positions of elite power and authority.

Scribes

The primary function of a scribe was to write stuff down, but to think of them solely as a sort of "secretary" would sell them short; scribes were more like lawyers. Scribes were very important people in the Old Testament who wrote and issued decrees in the name of

the king. They were very active in all affairs of state, probably given their ability to write and their more formalized educations.

Chief Priests

The chief priests were either men from priestly families who held positions of stature or those who had been entrusted with authority among the priests.

Sanhedrin

A council of seventy Jewish men who acted as judges. The Sanhedrin would have been their version of our US Supreme Court on matters of religious practice and theological disagreement.

Pharisees

The term *Pharisee* comes from a Hebrew word that means "separate." In the time of Jesus, they were the popular religious political party (see John 7:48). What we need to understand about the Pharisees is that they were very legalistic; they separated themselves from other Jews. While the intentions seemed pure, their religion was more about form and function and not about surrender or humility. They were very self-righteous (see Matthew 9; Luke 18), and Jesus laid into them (check out Matthew 12:9; 16:1–4). The Pharisees "supplemented" the Law by their own traditions, which took the Law an unnecessary step or two further.

Sadducees

The Sadducees were also a Jewish sect. They probably began as a by-product of the Greek philosophy that was pervading the Mediterranean world before the time of Jesus. The first time we see them in the gospel, they came out to challenge John the Baptist (see Matthew 3). Jesus calls them hypocrites (see Matthew 16). What we need to understand about the Sadducees (which makes them different from the Pharisees) is that they denied the doctrine of the Resurrection, denied the existence of angels or spirits, and denied the obligation to follow oral traditions (beyond what was written down). After the

destruction of Jerusalem in about AD 70, we don't hear much more about the Sadducees.

WORD PLAY

In the Psalm we hear the word *sanctuary*, which is a common word among us Catholics. From the Latin *sanctuarium*, the word means "holy place." The sanctuary in our parishes is supposed to be an area clearly "set apart" from the rest of the parish. It is where the altar and the timeless sacrifice of Christ is offered.

JOURNAL

1. Have you ever had a moment like Jeremiah—one of those, "Seriously, God?" moments? What happened that led you there? How did God respond?

2. Is there something (or maybe someone) who is causing you suffering in your life right now? What is it? Why is it hurting you?

3. Jesus tells his disciples, "If any man would come after me, let him deny himself and take up his cross and follow me" (Mt 16:24). How does this apply to your life and this specific area of suffering?

4. Why must we see suffering as Christ does and not as the world? How might the world's view of suffering be detrimental to your faith?

CHALLENGE FOR THE WEEK

Whenever you are tempted to complain about this suffering you experience in your daily life, take a moment to prayerfully give that suffering (and everything you are feeling) to God. Ask him, in that moment, to guide your mind and heart, that you may be charitable in how you speak and act and grateful for all that you do have. And ask him, above all, for the peace of heart you need to trust that he will protect and provide for you always.

Love Does No Evil

Twenty-Third Sunday in Ordinary Time

OPENING PRAYER

Lord, you are so good. Thank you for your love and for teaching us how to love. Open my heart to you today so that I may always love my neighbor (and myself) well. Amen.

> **First Reading:** Ezekiel 33:7–9
> **Responsorial Psalm:** Psalm 95:1–2, 6–9
> **Second Reading:** Romans 13:8–10
> **Gospel:** Matthew 18:15–20

BEYOND WORDS

"Live and let live" is a popular philosophy in modern culture. It's the idea that the most respectful thing we can do and be as human beings is exceedingly tolerant—refusing to speak into anyone's decisions, way of life, or personal beliefs. While we absolutely must respect the dignity and beliefs of others, is that really loving someone? If you see someone abusing another and justifying it with their personal belief, are you really required to remain silent? At what point does natural law and revealed truth supersede social awkwardness or the fear of "judgment" from others?

This week's readings demonstrate that God is not okay with his children sitting on the sidelines with hands clasped over their eyes. No, to follow God means to know Truth and to share that Truth when the time presents itself. This first reading from Ezekiel is a great example of this point, where the listener is warned that if they fail to instruct the wicked, they, too, will be held accountable by God. Put simply—knowledge is power, and a failure to share it carried a consequence. The psalmist warns us not to harden our hearts to God's truth and then reminds us of what happened to those who did (you can read more about that in the Behind the Scenes section). Jesus

instructs us to bring up transgressions and wrongdoings of another, first to them but then, if necessary, to the authority (the Church) out of love. Christ loves us too much to allow us to sit in our death called sin. St. Paul is so emphatic about it that he recaps the commandments but couches them in the command to love one another. He points out that love actually fulfills the Law (the commandments of God).

We are called to love one another, but that never means turning a blind eye to another's sin. Allowing someone to persist in selfishness and death is not love but the exact opposite. Part of love is truth, and if we fail to share that truth, we are not really fully loving another, are we? "Live and let live" is based on the premise that we want the other person to actually *live,* and without Christ we are not really living; we are merely breathing.

RELATED FACT

The name *Ezekiel* means "God strengthens." The entire book of Ezekiel is forty-eight chapters long containing almost thirty thousand words.

BEHIND THE SCENES

In this week's psalm we hear the warning not to "harden your hearts as at Mer'ibah, as in the day at Massah in the wilderness." Obviously, very few twenty-first-century souls sitting in the pews will understand what they are hearing or singing when these references come up.

Mer'ibah and Massah were important in the time of Moses as the Israelites were wandering for forty years in the desert. Mer'ibah means "contention" or "strife," while Massah translates to "testing." These two locations (you can read about them in Exodus 17:1–7 and Numbers 20:2–13) were places that the *children* of God acted more like the *brats* of God. In each site, the Israelites complained to God for the lack of water in the desert, and in each location—although they didn't deserve it—God miraculously provided water for them.

Just as God provided water for his children in the literal desert, he provides the Living Water—Jesus—to his children now wandering through the spiritual desert (Earth) seeking the Promised Land of heaven.

WORD PLAY

The word *wicked* that we hear in the first reading from Ezekiel comes from the word *wicca*, which is Old English for "witch," meaning "evil" or "morally wrong."

JOURNAL

1. When is a time that you have shared the truth of God confidently? How did it go?

2. When is a time that you struggled to share the truth of God at all? What happened? If you had that opportunity again, what would you do differently?

3. How can we love someone well without encouraging their sin? Is there a specific person in your life you need to learn how to love better?

4. In his Letter to the Romans, St. Paul says, "Love is the fulfilling of the law" (Rom 13:10). What does this mean? How does it apply to your own life?

CHALLENGE FOR THE WEEK

Take some time to reflect on your answer to Journal question 2, specifically the "what would you do differently" part. Perhaps you recognized the need for courage, confidence, the right words, the right timing, or a loving tone. Whatever it is, this week, pray specifically for the temperament or gift you need to present the truth lovingly to others when they need to hear it.

Lord, Have Mercy

Twenty-Fourth Sunday in Ordinary Times

OPENING PRAYER

Lord God, sometimes I am so complacent in my faith. I don't really work hard, and I take for granted the peace I do have in my life. Please give me the clarity this week to see in what areas of my life I have found myself comfortable. Please help me to grow in faith this week, although it may cause me a little bit of discomfort. Amen.

First Reading: Sirach 27:30–28:7
Responsorial Psalm: Psalm 103:1–2, 3–4, 9–10, 11–12
Second Reading: Romans 14:7–9
Gospel: Matthew 18:21–35

BEYOND WORDS

How badly do you want the Lord to forgive your sins? How far are you willing to go for God's mercy?

Usually the answers to those questions are directly proportional to how seriously we take and view our own sins. If we view our sins as deadly and our salvation as a work in progress, we will seek the Lord, daily, and in the confessional, often. If, however, we view our sins as "not that big a deal" or "not as bad as other people's sins," we will grow slothful in our faith life and prayer. We won't seek God's mercy and, in turn, won't readily offer mercy to those who have wronged us.

Sirach is as practical and wise as ever in this first reading. We are given a glimpse into the fate that awaits those so filled with anger. The "tighter we hug" wrath and anger, the more we open ourselves up to God's just vengeance. The Lord is kind and merciful, though, as we hear in the psalm, so where would vengeance come into this? When we refuse to offer mercy to others, we close ourselves off to God's mercy toward us, as we see in the gospel. We must "forgive from our hearts," we are reminded, because in doing so we are *with* the Lord. And those who "live for the Lord" and "die for the Lord" *"are the Lord's."*

Thank the Lord this week for his great mercy by offering mercy to those in your life who least deserve it but most need it.

RELATED FACT

The psalm's phrase "as far as the east is from the west" is a Hebrew expression referring to the rising and setting sun. It was a literal reference demonstrating the greatest visual distance from one end of the Earth to the other, offering an example of how far God has placed us away from our sins and transgressions through his grace.

BEHIND THE SCENES

The book of Sirach is a hidden jewel within the Bible. Many have never read it, but its contents are of great value. Known as a *deutero-canonical* book, Sirach appears in the Catholic Bible but is omitted in Protestant and non-Catholic translations (unless it is included in what is called the *apocrypha*). Over the centuries, some have attempted to claim that the Catholic Church somehow "added" books to the Bible, but that is historically unfounded and absolutely untrue. There is not sufficient space here to explain why there is a difference in the number of books between Catholic and non-Catholic Bibles. Suffice to say, the Catholic Bible containing seventy-three books was the unilateral and accepted Bible for well over one thousand years. It was not until the Protestant Reformation that non-Catholic followers then *removed* books from the Catholic Bible, taking their number down to sixty-six books.

All that being said, the book of Sirach was originally written in Hebrew about two hundred years before Christ and was translated into Greek by the author's grandson. Filled with timeless wisdom, memorable sayings, and pithy insights, Sirach is like a timeline of Tweets over two thousand years before Twitter even came into existence. Much like the book of Proverbs, Sirach is a great book you can pick up anytime, turn to a random page, and see just how much you have in common with your ancestors from two millennia ago. Wisdom is never outdated.

WORD PLAY

From the Latin *hominaticum, homage* (from the gospel reading) means to publicly honor, respect, or praise another.

JOURNAL

1. Where have you grown complacent in your life? What do you hold on to selfishly?

2. If Jesus were to appear today and ask you to give up those things so that you had the room in your life to follow him freely, would you?

3. What about anger? Do you hold on to that selfishly? Why?

4. If God is already merciful and forgiving, why must we also be merciful and forgiving of others? Explain. How does this apply to your life?

CHALLENGE FOR THE WEEK

Sometimes we focus on the sins of others because we are avoiding (perhaps, inadvertently) our own sins. This week, take some time to go to Confession. It is only when we empty ourselves of our own selfishness that we can love others best. Because it is when we are emptied that God's mercy that love can fill us up and, in turn, permeate every interaction we have with others.

Look at It This Way

Twenty-Fifth Sunday in Ordinary Time

OPENING PRAYER

Almighty God, you are all-knowing and so good. Please teach me how to trust you more and more each day, and help me listen well to your plans for my life. May I be assured in knowing that your plans are good, and you will take care of me always. Amen.

> **First Reading:** Isaiah 55:6–9
> **Responsorial Psalm:** Psalm 145:2–3, 8–9, 17–18
> **Second Reading:** Philippians 1:20c–24, 27a
> **Gospel:** Matthew 20:1–16a

BEYOND WORDS

The Christian life is often a battle for perspective. Jesus often challenges us to see things not from an earthly perspective but from a heavenly one. The word *perspective* is interesting in that its definition is also an invitation. From the Latin, the word *per,* meaning "through," and the word *specere,* meaning "to look," join to form *perspicere,* inviting us to "look through" a situation to gain proper perspective.

We are told this week that "the last will be first, and the first last." Our Lord enjoys a good turn of phrase to make his point to the listeners. It's illogical, though, at first hearing, isn't it? Are the last ever really first on Earth? Don't we cheer for the gold medalist and forget the person in last place? Yes, we do—on Earth.

God himself is standing in our midst reminding us that heavenly glory and earthly glory are far different. We should not desire personal attention or accolades but, rather, salvation for all (as we see in the gospel). We should view the little "deaths" and sacrifices in our lives as joys that will help us truly, finally live as St. Paul points out in his Letter to the Romans. How often we get hung up on earthly things

that don't really matter; heaven is what matters! It is only when we really seek the Lord in prayer and ask his thoughts to become our thoughts that we can take on a divine perspective, seeing *through* earthly mishaps and problems and allowing the peace of heaven to breathe into and keep calm our earthly hearts and minds.

RELATED FACT

The "days" in Jesus's time were divided into several "hours" during the day and four "watches" at night. The daytime hours began at 6:00 a.m. and lasted until 6:00 p.m. Thus, 9:00 a.m. was the "third" hour, noon was the "sixth" hour, and so forth. We hear these time designations during the account of our Lord's Crucifixion. This is also why you might remember that the apostles were on the boat in the storm during the fourth "watch" of night, as we discussed several weeks back.

BEHIND THE SCENES

Over the centuries, many saints and scholars have weighed in on this parable from Matthew's gospel. They have rightly noted that the different laborers and their timely responses to God's call can be likened to the different "times" in our lives that we begin to follow God (i.e., "dawn" workers are the people who begin following God early on in life, "5:00 p.m." workers are those who come to know him in their older years, etc.). The point is that regardless of when people start walking with the Lord, all have the chance to know his mercy and love.

Scholars point out, too, the perceived "injustice" the landowner has committed: offering the same full wage to those who worked only an hour, while others slaved away in the blazing heat all day. What they (and, often, we) consider injustice is actually incredible generosity on the part of the landowner. Similarly, should we be annoyed if an atheist has a conversion a short time before their death and gets to enjoy heaven the same as someone who's followed God their entire life? Do we desire their salvation or only our reward?

One of the interesting subplots, however, is that this is a parable meant not just to open our eyes to the great mercy and inconceivably generous love of God but, also, to reveal the darkness that resides in our own hearts. Even if the day-long workers' argument were valid, that they had worked much harder, the anger they felt toward the landowner was unmerited. We all benefit from the mercy of God. We all enjoy the promise of salvation, provided that we heed the call when it comes to us and cooperate with God's grace. Rather than begrudging latecomers to the table of the Lord, we ought to relish in the fact that we've been seated here for so long and do everything we can to invite as many more souls as possible to come and feast at the heavenly banquet.

WORD PLAY

A *denarius* was a Roman coin that equaled about a day's wage for someone doing manual labor. The New American Bible with the revised New Testament—read at Mass—refers to "daily wage," while other translations (like the Revised Standard Version) use the exact word "denarius."

JOURNAL

1. Have you ever been in last place or felt as though no one noticed your accomplishments? How did it make you feel?

2. How does understanding that God sees and knows all things change how you feel?

3. In our second reading from Isaiah, God says, "As the heavens are higher than the earth, so are my ways higher than your ways" (Is 55:9). What does this mean?

4. Is there an area of your life where you feel the Lord is asking you to trust that he knows how hard you're working, even though you don't feel as though you're getting the recognition you deserve? If so, what area is that?

CHALLENGE FOR THE WEEK

Is there someone you often compare yourself to? Perhaps you wonder why they get more praise and recognition. Maybe a sibling or coworker or someone else you have watched with a bit of envy? Whoever that person is, commit to praying for them and their salvation every day this week.

Actions Speak Louder

Twenty-Sixth Sunday in Ordinary Time

OPENING PRAYER

Lord, sometimes I am so selfish. I go about my day, thinking only of myself, and lose sight of the beautiful gift of those around me, most importantly, you! Please help me to regain my sight of the least and the lowly. May I have your eyes and heart in all of my interactions, today and always. Amen.

> **First Reading:** Ezekiel 18:25–28
> **Responsorial Psalm:** Psalm 25:4–5, 8–10, 14
> **Second Reading:** Philippians 2:1–11
> **Gospel:** Matthew 21:28–32

BEYOND WORDS

How does one measure love? Is it by the number of times you say it to your loved one? Is it by the number of romantic gestures or love notes or "blowing kisses" emojis used in text messages?

Of course not. Because what love requires is far greater than what words can achieve.

It's easy to say, "I love you," but living it out requires a whole different level of surrender. This week's gospel demonstrates this point beautifully. Talk is cheap. The son who says he'll serve the father but fails to is outshone by the one who initially declines but eventually comes to his senses, rises, and heads out. Ezekiel expands on this point, demonstrating how those who live a virtuous life—not those who merely talk about it—will receive their reward, while those who sin do not act in line with the Lord's way and will suffer the consequence. Our actions speak louder than our words because actions matter.

This really is the root of the Incarnation that St. Paul is explaining to the people in Philippi in the second reading. God is not a "do as

ORDINARY TIME

179

I say, not as I do" kind of God. No, God says, "Do what I did." God humbled himself by "emptying himself" and "becoming obedient to the point of death . . . on a cross." The Cross goes far beyond words. Jesus didn't just say, "I love you," to the Father or to us; he lived it out with every action, and his Cross was the exclamation point. It's not enough for us to say that we love the Lord; it ought to be readily visible in our daily actions and crosses. If there is no willingness to sacrifice for the other, it is not true love.

RELATED FACT

Note that the second reading from Philippians states, "Every knee should bow, in heaven and on the earth and under the earth" (Phil 2:10). In ancient Israel, these were considered the three "realms" of life, and this verse shows that Christ is Lord over all three, demonstrating his authority and sovereignty over all of creation.

BEHIND THE SCENES

This week's gospel is like a divine "mic drop" on Jesus's part. It's no secret that the chief priests and elders considered themselves the holiest men around. As Jesus interacts with them, time and time again, his message is one of warnings about their pride and encouragement to repent and humble themselves. Out of mercy, Jesus is knocking them down a few pegs, hoping that their hard hearts would break, opening themselves up to the God they claimed to know.

What makes this parable shocking is not merely that Jesus puts tax collectors and prostitutes on par with the first son, who was to be praised. (Yes, tax collectors and prostitutes were considered the absolute worst of the worst when it came to sinners of the time. Yet once they have repented, much like the first son, they are to be praised for their faithfulness.) No, this parable is shocking not because of God's great mercy nor the sinners' humility but because of the implication it makes to the prideful souls listening.

The chief priests and elders are put on notice by Jesus here. The ones who think they are on top of the ladder have actually walked

beneath it. Jesus is equating them with the second son who, in essence, had agreed to follow the Father's commands but failed to do so. By firmly establishing these self-proclaimed "holy men" with the second son, Jesus is teaching us that our true discipleship is about actions and not merely words. At the same time, it is a stern warning to the chief priests and elders to repent and change their ways because their pride would be their downfall in the end.

WORD PLAY

Iniquity is immoral behavior, usually especially selfish and unfair. It comes from the Latin *iniquitas*, meaning "not just" (*in* means "not," and *aequus* means "equal"), and appears almost 150 times within the Bible.

JOURNAL

1. What does it mean to "empty yourself," as St. Paul says Jesus did on the Cross (see Philippians 2:7)?

2. How can you "empty yourself" more in your own life? What does that look like for you at home or at work?

3. Who do you need to love better with your actions this week? Your spouse, kids, coworkers, etc.?

4. Jesus calls us to carry our own crosses as he did. What is your cross this week?

CHALLENGE FOR THE WEEK

How have you sacrificed recently for your immediate family? This week, with humility, do one act of kindness for each of them. As you offer this sacrifice, pray for them.

Make Your Requests Known to God

Twenty-Seventh Sunday in Ordinary Time

OPENING PRAYER

Almighty God, I thank you, today, for the gift of growth. For, if it weren't for our hardships and trials, we wouldn't fully appreciate how good you are. Please teach me how to grow well in my daily trials, especially through the gifts of patience and fortitude. Amen.

First Reading: Isaiah 5:1–7
Responsorial Psalm: Psalm 80:9, 12–16, 19–20
Second Reading: Philippians 4:6–9
Gospel: Matthew 21:33–43

BEYOND WORDS

Making wine is a long and arduous process. Long before a bottle of wine ever gets opened, many seasons have passed, and hundreds of steps have taken place. The land must be procured, the soil must be right—tilled, and prepared—before the seeds are ever planted. We hear a little about the process in the first reading from Isaiah and, again, mirrored in the gospel. The wine press must be hewn, and a watchtower must be built, and this doesn't even speak into the need for proper weather conditions, the laborious work of the harvest, and the pressing and seemingly never-ending wait during the fermentation process. All in all, it takes years to achieve something truly amazing when it comes to wine. The same can be said of the Christian.

The soil of our hearts must be right for the seed of God's Word to take root and thrive. It is only through our connectedness to God (the vine and the branches) and through building our lives on Christ, the cornerstone (the gospel), that we can withstand the difficulties of the season. Sometimes we suffer. Sometimes our prayer lives are

arid. Sometimes we are persecuted like Christ was (and still is) by others. We, like the grapes, undergo a great deal of duress but, in time, those are the grapes that produce the best juice and the sweetest taste. Through all these ups and downs and seasons of life, if we remain connected to him who is true and that which is "honorable, just, pure, lovely, gracious, etc.," as we hear from St. Paul, then we will know peace and we will, in time, bear great fruit. It is in "making our requests known to God" that we come to trust in his plan, his timing, and, ultimately, his will for our lives.

RELATED FACT

The cornerstone was considered the most important stone in a building project. Placed at the intersection of two walls, the cornerstone joined and solidified both walls. Ironically, stones that were "rejected" previously were tossed aside because their appearance was imperfect or they were considered useless in a building project. The builders of the Temple that Jesus refers to in the gospel were the chief priests, who rejected Christ—who proves to be the cornerstone of the new Temple (the Church).

BEHIND THE SCENES

As previously stated, the word *parable* comes from the Greek word that means "comparison." The key to understanding parables begins with, first, identifying what each person or element represents. In this parable of the wicked tenants, for instance, the following can be identified:

- The landowner is God.
- The vineyard is Jerusalem.
- The tenants are the chief priests, elders, and other religious leaders.
- The servants are the Old Testament prophets.
- The son is (obviously) Jesus.
- The other tenants will be the future leaders of the Church.

Now with that straight, reread the parable in light of these clarifications, and pay attention to a few details: What happened to most of the prophets in the Old Testament? Yes, they were killed just like the servants. Where was the son killed? Outside the vineyard. Given that the vineyard represents Jerusalem, it's worthy of mention that Calvary/Golgotha is a location technically found "outside" the city walls or limits. The tenants are punished by death when Jerusalem is overrun and the Temple destroyed in AD 70. Note, too, that it is the chief priests and elders, themselves, who recommend this punishment when Christ asks them what should come of the tenants.

One last fascinating detail to this entire dialogue is the location in which it is taking place. This scene transpires after Jesus's triumphant entry into Jerusalem. Jesus—the stone which the builders rejected—is having this conversation with them in front of the Temple, which was still under construction. It was the chief priests who were in charge of this Temple building project. They would have been the ones to have selected the cornerstone and to have rejected others. Just as the tenants rejected the son in the parable, just days after this interaction, they would reject the Son, cast him out of the city, and have him put to death unjustly.

WORD PLAY

The Gospel speaks of "vintage time." *Vintage* is a wine-making term referring to the time of year grapes were harvested for wine making. The term comes from the Latin *vindemia*, where *vinum* means "wine" and *demere* means "remove."

JOURNAL

1. What season do you feel like you are in right now? A season of great harvest, a season of growth, a season of waiting, etc.? Explain.

2. Have you ever experienced a time of great anxiety in your life? If so, what caused that anxiety? What did you find that helped to

relieve that anxiety? Is this a healthy practice you can incorporate into your daily life?

3. St. Paul says, "Have no anxiety about anything, but in everything, by prayer and supplication with thanksgiving, let your requests be known to God" (Phil 4:6). Why does he give this advice? What do his words teach us?

CHALLENGE FOR THE WEEK

Pick a project that you've wanted to do for a while (perhaps it is an art project, a fitness goal, or to learn a new skill). Plan out this project this week and get started on it. As you work on this project, use it as a time to prayerfully recognize the patience and diligence it takes to go from the initial plan to the finished project. Share this project with a friend, and ask for their accountability and encouragement along the way.

God Gives Everything We Need

Twenty-Eighth Sunday in Ordinary Time

OPENING PRAYER

I can trust in you, Lord. I can trust in you.

(Pray this prayer until you believe it, even if it takes years...)

> **First Reading:** Isaiah 25:6–10a
> **Responsorial Psalm:** Psalm 23:1–6
> **Second Reading:** Philippians 4:12–14, 19–20
> **Gospel:** Matthew 22:1–14

BEYOND WORDS

Will God be there for me when I need him, when I can't feel him, in my suffering, in my loneliness? Will God bring justice to all the injustices in this life? Can I count on him when I am at my weakest?

These are common questions in life, regardless of age, upbringing, or family of origin. Is God about *us* or only about himself? Consider the promises set forth in the first reading. Here we see God "providing for all peoples" with a choice banquet that not only serves the need but far exceeds it. It is accompanied by a promise of justice and mercy "wiping away the tears from every face" and the glory of salvation by him. Likewise, we are told by the psalmist that we will be invited not only to visit the house of the Lord but to actually "live in the house of the Lord."

It's for this reason that the gospel parable is so stunning. God is opening his wedding banquet and home to *all*, not just the VIP list. We all have an invitation to join him in the celebration. He wants not only to know us more intimately but to feed us in the process (cue the Eucharistic foreshadowing)! It's with this knowledge that St. Paul tells the Philippians to rejoice and give God glory because no matter the circumstance, whether you are hungry or well-fed, God is with you; he will fulfill your needs *and then some*.

RELATED FACT

Scholars debate what exactly was the "wedding garment." Most believe it is an allusion to a clean robe or tunic as opposed to work clothes (think "Sunday best"). Revelation 19 discusses the wedding garment as a symbol of our righteous deeds and holy life, which St. Jerome (in his commentary on Matthew's gospel) agreed with and expounded upon.

BEHIND THE SCENES

At the time of Jesus, weddings were a huge affair (some would argue far more so than even today). Customarily, two invitations would be sent: one inviting people to the forthcoming ceremony and reception and another one alerting them that the banquet was now prepared and to come immediately.

When the guests who had RSVP'd "yes" decline their invitation (some even beating the messengers), the king is understandably shocked and outraged. He sends troops for payback and burns their homes and cities. Then he invites *all* to the feast (even people the king and groom do not yet know)—the forgotten, the beggars, the outcasts. You know how the story ends with one of these late invitees arriving but not dressed appropriately.

Christ, the bridegroom, often uses wedding imagery and analogies to describe and unpack the mystery of God's love and of the kingdom. This parable is rather straightforward, though, setting Jesus as the bridegroom and God the Father as the king. The messengers, like the prophets, announce the forthcoming banquet, and many are mistreated. When Jesus comes on the scene proclaiming that the kingdom of God (the wedding banquet) is at hand, we see the invitation extended to all (the bad and the good, the Jews and the Gentiles, the rich and the poor, etc.). The final moment—detailing a guest not clothed in the wedding garment (righteous, good deeds)—is a stern reminder to us that while all are invited to heaven, not all will see it. Actions matter. Decisions carry consequences. Some people in our lives have declined the invitation to know the Lord, others have rejected it, and still others have waged war against his followers and messengers. In the end, we will be judged and included or excluded based upon the lives we led and the decisions we made. Many are called, indeed, but, sadly, only few will be chosen.

WORD PLAY

From the Latin *abundantia*, *abundance* means "overflowing." The blessings from God, as described by St. Paul in the second reading, are abundant, and so is a life living in his grace.

JOURNAL

1. Why is trust in God difficult? Explain.

2. St. Paul says, "I can do all things in him who strengthens me" (Phil 4:13). What does this mean?

3. Have you seen this verse come to light in your own life? Explain.

4. What is one area of your life you feel is lacking in some way? How can you ask God, this week, to fill that area?

CHALLENGE FOR THE WEEK

Write out a prayer to God telling him what it is you need most right now and asking him to provide for you in whatever way he knows you need. Pray this prayer every day this week.

In God We Trust

Twenty-Ninth Sunday in Ordinary Time

OPENING PRAYER

God, thank you for knowing more about what I need than I know myself. Teach me how to lean more on you than I do myself and others. May I trust that you have my best intentions in mind at all times and that you know how to take care of me. May I never fear you. May I always truly believe that you can be trusted. Amen.

First Reading: Isaiah 45:1, 4–6
Responsorial Psalm: Psalm 96:1, 3–5, 7–10
Second Reading: 1 Thessalonians 1:1–5b
Gospel: Matthew 22:15–21

BEYOND WORDS

Ask a child to plug in a lamp, and they know where to go and what to do. Ask that child where the power comes from, and most will point to the socket as the source of the power. Few kids, however, would be able to explain to you the true source—be it a power plant or renewable energy—where the power *actually* comes from. They know the destination far better than its source.

The same can be said of the earthly rulers mentioned in this week's readings. In the first reading we hear about Cyrus, the king of Persia, who was given his station and allowed his earthly authority by God, "though [Cyrus] knew him [God] not." Similarly, in the gospel, as the Pharisees set out to upset Christ, they posit the question to him about the authority of God versus the authority of Caesar, representing the Roman rule and oppression they found themselves under. Again, here we see that while Rome might have earthly rule, eternal dominion and authority reside solely within God. We see the distinction being drawn between worldly power and true power,

189

the power that comes in the Holy Spirit (as we are told in the second reading), that which is available to us and which convicts us.

While those in leadership, be it global or local, may not recognize that their power is entrusted to them by others or from above, we who are called to lead in the faith know to "give the Lord glory and honor," as the psalm says, because the only power we enjoy is that which he grants us in his mercy. We know the Source of all power and light—while some others only see the socket.

RELATED FACT

The phrase "In God We Trust" first appeared on US currency (the two-cent coin) in 1864; the motto did not appear on paper currency until 1957.

BEHIND THE SCENES

The coin in question in this week's gospel was a silver Roman denarius, worth roughly one day's wage. One side of the coin bore the image of Tiberius Caesar, who served as the emperor of Rome from about AD 14 to AD 37. The other side of the coin bore the inscription "high priest." All the Jews of the time would have been offended by this solemn and respected title of "high priest" being claimed by the "pagan" Romans with their false gods, especially the Pharisees, who are ironically using this to try to trap the Lord.

As we know from Genesis chapter 1, we are "made in God's image and likeness." Jesus turns the tables on the Pharisees (and, by extension, the Romans) when he declares that the coin, bearing Caesar's image, belongs to the Romans and ought to be given to them. All human beings then, by extension, made in God's image belong to the one, true God and are to be given (or to give ourselves back) to our Creator and Father.

WORD PLAY

The word *hypocrite*, used by Jesus in the gospel, is the same word in Greek (*hupokritēs*) that is used for "actor."

JOURNAL

1. Is it difficult to allow God to rule in your own life? Why or why not?

2. In what ways can you share the true Source of all power and light with those around you?

3. Jesus challenges the Pharisees to "render therefore to Caesar the things that are Caesar's, and to God the things that are God's" (Mt 22:21). What does this mean?

4. How does this challenge apply directly to your life? Explain.

CHALLENGE FOR THE WEEK

Is there something in your life (perhaps an object, habit, friend) that you allow to rule your life more than God? Today, take some time to prayerfully consider what this is. We all have something; it may be small. This week, challenge yourself to give up that "something" that causes you to lose sight of the true Source of power and light.

All Yours

Thirtieth Sunday in Ordinary Time

OPENING PRAYER

When all else fades, Lord, you are there. When I have nothing left, you are my strength. Thank you, Lord, for your incredible gift of love. May I learn how (albeit, slowly) to love you and all those I encounter just as you love me. Amen.

> **First Reading:** Exodus 22:20–26
> **Responsorial Psalm:** Psalm 18:2–4, 47, 51
> **Second Reading:** 1 Thessalonians 1:5c–10
> **Gospel:** Matthew 22:34–40

BEYOND WORDS

Have you ever "ranked" the Ten Commandments from the least to most important to follow? Does not committing murder really deserve to rank up there with "keeping holy the sabbath," for instance? Even in the time of Jesus, we see the Pharisees and Sadducees asking for a list in order of importance. There were so many commandments to follow, after all, and so few ways to "trap" the Lord into violating the Law with his answers.

Being far too smart for his opponents, the Lord summarizes all the commandments in just two (which you can read more about in the following sections). In doing so, Jesus picks up where Moses left off in his instructions to offer love and mercy to your neighbor. How does one follow the Ten Commandments perfectly? It all begins with loving God with everything you are and everything you have. This is why St. Paul told those in Thessalonica to become "imitators of us and of the Lord," not because they were egotistical but, instead, because they were trying to offer a living witness of a new way of life—a life bent on knowing, loving, and serving God and neighbor. They were "all in" and "all his" and were encouraging other followers to follow suit and do the same. We are to have a preferential option and heart, too, for those who are most in need and most vulnerable—namely, widows and orphans. Throughout scripture we hear "widows and orphans" placed together because the two represented a cross section who could not take care of or provide for themselves. God is seen repeatedly in both the Old and New Testaments as a champion of those without a voice (like children in the womb, still today), and loving the Lord means loving all life, even the alienated and the seemingly forgotten.

RELATED FACT

The first reading from Exodus mentions taking "your neighbor's garment in pledge." The cloak in question was likely a rectangular garment that functioned both as outer clothing and as a blanket (at night). For the poor, this was normally their only and most valuable possession. They would give it to someone as a pledge of repayment in the future, in hopes of getting it back (much like modern pawnbrokers).

BEHIND THE SCENES

Much has been written over the centuries about both the Ten Commandments and the "greatest commandment" as we hear in this week's gospel. Often when these themes are discussed, people nitpick the little details so much that they miss the big picture of what Jesus is actually saying here. Some have tried to advance the notion that Jesus is, in a way, "rejecting" the Ten Commandments of Moses in favor of a somewhat "reduced" two commandments of love. The misnomer is that if people just love (which is a nebulous term in and of itself), then all will be good in God's eyes.

The problem with this type of oversimplification is that it doesn't take the whole of scripture into account.

First, there are two "sets" of commandments within the ten entrusted to Moses atop Mount Sinai. The first three help us to love God with our whole being (heart, soul, and mind). The next seven

aid us in loving our neighbor as our self. In this way, Jesus has not reduced as much as recapped in a simpler way. Second, note that Jesus tells us "the whole law and the prophets depend on these two" in the verse that follows. In other words, no other commandment holds weight or can be properly followed if these two (in essence, ten) are not heeded, observed, and obeyed. Those who attempt to seek loopholes—picking and choosing the commandments that best fit their own agenda—will be disappointed to find out that these two greatest commandments recap the ten and are the foundation for everything we believe and do. This is a reminder to seek the Lord and never the loophole.

WORD PLAY

The term *alien* referred to anyone from a foreign land. The word comes to us from the Latin *alienus*, meaning "belonging to another."

JOURNAL

1. Why does Jesus give this commandment to us as the greatest of all commandments?

2. What does this say about how we must approach the other commandments?

3. Is it difficult for you to love God with all of your heart and all of your mind (see Luke 10:27)? Why? What makes it difficult?

4. In what ways can you love God or your neighbor better? Explain.

CHALLENGE FOR THE WEEK

Have you ever questioned God on the Ten Commandments like the Pharisees did with Jesus? Write down any questions you have about the faith, and take them to a trusted "authority" in your parish (e.g., your pastor, deacon, religious sister, RCIA director, etc.) and ask him or her the questions. Commit to finding the answers and trusting in the Lord as you do it.

Till the Ends of the Earth

Feast of All Saints

OPENING PRAYER

Dear God, you are merciful and good in all of your ways. I pray in thanksgiving for the great call you have given us to be in total and complete union with you. God, I ask for a brave and courageous heart to follow this call by fearlessly living a life of discipleship. Send your Spirit upon me so that I may conform my way to yours and, in every action, give glory to you. Amen.

> **First Reading:** Revelation 7:2–4, 9–14
> **Responsorial Psalm:** Psalm 24:1bc–2, 1–4ab, 5–6
> **Second Reading:** 1 John 3:1–3
> **Gospel:** Matthew 5:1–12a

BEYOND WORDS

There is a popular modern misconception that "all roads lead to heaven." Theologically and spiritually speaking, this concept is the anti-Gospel. Repeatedly throughout his earthly ministry, Jesus speaks—and, more to the point, *warns* us—about the reality of heaven and hell. Not everyone will see heaven, no matter how badly God desires all souls to be saved.

That being said, as a Church we do not focus on damnation and hell but, rather, on salvation and heaven. On this day, when we celebrate the saints in heaven, we pause and reflect on the lives that our holy brothers and sisters in faith led while on Earth—lives of virtue and selflessness where love was seen in actions and not, merely, words. The gospel reminds us that the saints sought God, hungered for righteousness, offered mercy, and endured persecution. They are rejoicing and worshipping alongside the angels eternally (as seen in the first reading) because they, as the children of God (pointed out in the second reading), lived lives focused solely on him.

Everyone desires heaven, but most still live focused on Earth; they sacrifice the eternal for the temporary. We celebrate the saints because they had the awareness and humility to seek God in the face of temptation and personal struggles. We desire the "white robes" of righteousness that they are adorned in, hoping that one day we, too, will worship alongside the angels for all of eternity.

RELATED FACT

The first reading from Revelation mentions the holy ones "with palm branches in their hands." Palms (and palm trees) represent righteousness throughout scripture, due to the trees' strong and "straight" nature. Additionally, the act of waving palms dates back to the Jews' annual feast of Tabernacles, wherein they would hold them high and wave them as a sign of celebration and gratitude to the God of water and light for his faithfulness before the upcoming harvest.

BEHIND THE SCENES

Many misbelieve that the book of Revelation is merely a book filled with doom and gloom, pointing toward the end of the world. In reality, it is a book and message filled with hope—the same hope that its author (traditionally considered to be St. John Zebedee) echoes in his first letter (which we hear in the second reading).

The book of Revelation is written in a specific type of biblical literature—namely, apocalyptic. It is not really intended to be read as a historical narrative, like the gospels, for instance. Revelation communicates its message through imagery and symbolism. You will notice colors and numbers (and even creatures) that seem to be random, but all are used purposely, through the Holy Spirit's inspiration, to convey the message. Revelation is the kind of book that is subject to interpretation. That being said, it is therefore, naturally, going to be misinterpreted. Over the past two thousand years, countless laypeople have claimed to have "figured it out," but no one was completely sure. We are fortunate to have the guidance of the Church's Tradition

to help us unpack Revelation in the manner it was intended—free of fear, personal bias, or preconceived ideas.

WORD PLAY

Revelation comes from the Greek word *Apokalypsis*, which translates to "unveiling" or "pull back the veil." It is filled with wedding imagery, where Jesus Christ is the bridegroom, coming on a white horse (literally, check out Revelation 6 and 19), to save his bride, the Church.

JOURNAL

1. How do you imagine God would react to you standing before him? How would he greet you? What would he say to you?

2. When you think of the final judgment, what comes to mind? How does your idea differ from John's vision in Revelation?

3. What are your overall thoughts about this reading? How does this reading apply to your life?

CHALLENGE FOR THE WEEK

Step outside of your comfort zone this week and honor God in a new way (e.g., a good deed for a stranger, an authentic prayer, an act of love, etc.). Brainstorm and write that idea down, or tell a friend to hold you accountable.

Give Glory to His Name

Thirty-First Sunday in Ordinary Time

OPENING PRAYER

Lord, I desire to know you and be more like you. Today, teach me more about you and how you desire a unique relationship with me. Amen.

> **First Reading:** Malachi 1:14b–2:2b, 8–10
> **Responsorial Psalm:** Psalm 131:1–3
> **Second Reading:** 1 Thessalonians 2:7b–9, 13
> **Gospel:** Matthew 23:1–12

BEYOND WORDS

Knowing God is an attractive quality.

Consider that phrase. Think about people in your life who seem to really "know God" well. Perhaps it's your pastor or a religious sister you know. Maybe it's a coworker or radio host or your favorite speaker or author—that soul who just seems to *know God* on a level that you desire to know him.

Whoever the person, when we encounter souls who seem to have a deeper connection to the Lord, it is natural for us to be drawn to them. This is how so many preachers and leaders of different denominations can amass such huge followings, given their charism and giftedness. The problem, however, is when those who seem to "know" God lose touch with him on a personal level. The first reading gives a stern warning to those priests entrusted with preaching God's truth but who, instead, seek personal glory or comfort. Christ points to the Pharisees and Scribes—all learned men—who lord their knowledge of God's laws over the people, even though they are personally far from the Lord in their own hearts. The psalmist praises the children of God who find their peace solely in the proximity and care of their parent. St. Paul carries on that same imagery of a child beloved by

God and praises those followers who put up with hardship because they received not just "words about God" but the Word of God (Jesus). The Thessalonians are praised for their faithfulness to God and their humility in "knowing him." When we know who God is, we also discover who we are.

Ask yourself if people are drawn to you because of your faith, and then consider how well you turn that attention back to the Lord. For if people come to you seeking Christ and only find you, what have you accomplished? As Jesus reminds us, our leadership is rooted in our service: "The greatest among you must be your servant."

RELATED FACT

The name *Malachi* (first reading) means "my messenger" or "my angel." The book of Malachi has more than 1,300 words spread across four chapters.

BEHIND THE SCENES

Inevitably, when this gospel passage gets read, people begin to wonder why the Catholic Church refers to her priests as "fathers." It's important to point out that the very same verse also says that we are to call no man teacher, but for some reason that never seems to bother anyone. Also, if we were to really take this verse literally, we would never use the word *father* to refer to our own dads. So, is Jesus trying to make a point or just asking for us to make a universal change from *father* and *teacher* to *dad* and *instructor*? St. Paul, for example, refers to himself having become "a father" to the Corinthians through the Gospel that he preached (see 1 Corinthians 4:15). Is St. Paul just disregarding Christ's command?

In these verses, Jesus is speaking about the proper exercise of authority. This is clear from the fact that this teaching is given within the context of his criticizing the scribes and Pharisees for their hypocrisy as teachers and leaders of the Jewish people. (Read all of Matthew 23; Jesus really lets them have it.) Many of the scribes and Pharisees had developed a bad habit of dangling their power

and authority over others. They loved having these titles of "father" and "teacher" because they were used to setting themselves apart as superior to the rest of the Jews.

Jesus is reminding us that authority ultimately comes from God and that those who have received a position of leadership should exercise this leadership not for their own benefit but for the good of others. We can see that what Jesus is criticizing here is not the title itself, but those who seek these titles for their own sake or as a way of setting themselves up among the community as more important. The Church would agree with this criticism. It would be wrong for our priests to use their position of authority to take advantage of us since their position of authority is given for the sake of service to the Church. So, when we call our priests "Father," we are recognizing the fact that, through the authority given by Christ, they share in God's work of guiding and sustaining our spiritual lives. They do not take the place of God. In fact, their job is to guide and support us as we grow in spiritual maturity as faithful children of our true Father in heaven.

WORD PLAY

The gospel mentions the Pharisees widening their *phylacteries*. A phylactery was a small leather box that contained scripture verses and was worn upon the forehead and forearm during times of prayer. From the Greek *phulaktērion* for "amulet," the wider the box, the higher the public perception of one's piety and holiness. Jesus praises our humility but warns us of the pride behind wanting to "appear holy" to others.

JOURNAL

1. Is there someone in your life you admire because of this "attractiveness of faith"? Who is it, and what specifically do they convey that is attractive?

2. What is the difference between knowing about God and really, truly knowing him? Which relationship do you have?

3. In the first reading, why is Jesus so hard on the Pharisees? Is his frustration justified? Why?

4. When others look at you, do they see Christ? Explain. If Jesus were to have a conversation with you today about the honesty in which you live your life, what would he say?

CHALLENGE FOR THE WEEK

This week pay closer attention to what you say, how you act, and the promises you make. Did you *really* follow through on that promise? Did you *really* pray for that person you said you would pray for? Challenge yourself to follow through on your promises and to be a man or woman of your word!

Christic before Me

Thirty-Second Sunday in Ordinary Time

OPENING PRAYER

Lord, I realize I can do nothing on my own. Without you and your divine assistance, I could never accomplish sanctity. But I desire my home to be with you because that is how my heart was created—for you and you alone. You are the one who can satisfy my every longing. Yet sometimes I fail to see it this way and become lazy in my prayer. Today, I want this to be different. Please help me with this resolve. Amen.

> **First Reading:** Wisdom 6:12–16
> **Responsorial Psalm:** Psalm 63:2–8
> **Second Reading:** 1 Thessalonians 4:13–18
> **Gospel:** Matthew 25:1–13

BEYOND WORDS

These final few weeks of the liturgical year always bring with them more "intense" readings—such as the coming of the Lord in judgment and the end times. The readings are always quick to point out that, while "signs" and warnings will accompany Jesus's Second Coming (as we hear about in the second reading and the gospel), ultimately the intention is for all of us to be ready at any time.

If Christ were to come back tonight, would that fill you with peace or with a deep-seated desire to get to Confession?

Obviously, most of us would love to know the exact hour of Christ's coming so we could be receiving absolution as the skies opened and Christ came down on a cloud, but it doesn't work that way. If we are concerned about Christ's return, that usually signals changes we need to make in our lives. Are we the foolish bridesmaids who acted as though they had no idea the groom was coming, or are we the wise one who was prepared at all times? Do we have a vibrant

ONE SUNDAY AT A TIME

prayer life, do we frequent Confession and lean into the Mass, or do we only go to God when necessary or forced?

The first reading today might seem a bit out of thematic consistency when you read it, but upon a closer look we see something of an urgent pursuit. Wisdom (the Holy Spirit) is available to all who pursue it. Are we seeking the Lord passionately and urgently each day or only when we feel like it? Do we wake up and go to sleep with God on our mind and holiness the goal of our heart? If we are seeking the Lord, daily, we will be in good shape when the time comes. If we put Christ before ourselves and our own wants, and if our souls, as the psalmist says, are "thirsting for thee," we will find ourselves with full lamps joyfully awaiting the return of the One for whom we have longed.

RELATED FACT

"Trimming" their lamps was a method of ensuring that the wick to the lamp was not charred or in contact with the oil. It also ensured that the wick was long enough to hold the flame once lit.

BEHIND THE SCENES

The poignant nature of this week's gospel reading is often lost on modern readers because it references the Jewish matrimonial process in first-century Israel. Marriage happened in two "steps" back then. First, the families of the bride and groom would agree on terms for their kids to marry. This usually involved an exchange of money from the groom's family to the bride's family. Not to be seen as "buying," it was to make up for the money that would be lost due to the daughter no longer being able to work with and for the family and leaving them to live with the husband. After the terms were set, the couple was officially betrothed. Sometimes confused with engagement, this step actually meant the couple was legally married (hence, Joseph and Mary were actually married not just engaged). Following that betrothal and blessing, however, the bride continued to live with her parents as she prepared herself to become a wife and mother. At

the same time, the groom now went to build a new home for them. Sometimes this new home was an addition to his family's home, if it was not affordable or plausible to create an all-new dwelling place. In either case, it was only when the groom's father felt that the new dwelling was ready that the groom could then go and bring his new bride home.

When the time came, the groom and his groomsmen departed at sunset for the home of his bride, announcing the good news along the way and alerting guests that it was time to celebrate the wedding feast. The virgins' job was to be prepared to light the way (with their lanterns) on the way back, accompanying the bride and all the family members who (would have) joined into the procession by this point. The procession would culminate in a week-long party and feast (which is why running out of wine on "the third day" in Cana—see John 2:1–12—was so embarrassing).

The virgins running out of oil wasn't just embarrassing for them because they were unable to fulfill their duty, but it was even more depressing because they would have missed out on the banquet. It's a great lesson to be always prepared, so you don't find yourself on the outside looking in—literally.

WORD PLAY

To "keep vigil" means to remain awake, especially during times that are customary to be asleep. Additionally, *vigil* implies a need to keep watch or to pray for an impending enemy or visitor. It comes from the Latin *vigilia*, meaning "awake."

JOURNAL

1. How are you seeking the Lord, daily? Urgently and passionately or half-heartedly and apathetically?

2. If Christ were to come today, would you be ready? If Christ were to come tomorrow, what steps would you need to make to be ready?

3. What holds you back from seeking the Lord daily with urgency and passion? What changes can you make in your life to remedy this?

CHALLENGE FOR THE WEEK

This week, take some time to write a letter to God. In your letter, explain what changes you are willing to make in order to be ready for his Second Coming, and make a promise to him that you will do everything in your power to follow through on these changes. Conclude with a heartfelt prayer asking him for his wisdom and strength.

Sooner or Later

Thirty-Third Sunday in Ordinary Time

OPENING PRAYER

Quiet your mind and heart for a moment and consider one area you need more trust in God—perhaps it's your trust in his plan for peace within your family or friends, or your trust in his plan for your life—whatever it is, offer that area to him, and then pray these words with this prayer in mind: Jesus, I trust in you. Jesus, I trust in you. Jesus, I trust in you. Amen.

> **First Reading:** Proverbs 31:10–13, 19–20, 30–31
> **Responsorial Psalm:** Psalm 128:1–5
> **Second Reading:** 1 Thessalonians 5:1–6
> **Gospel:** Matthew 25:14–30

BEYOND WORDS

Saying that you can truly trust another person is one of the highest compliments that can be paid. Think about the people in your life who you trust completely, with everything: your fears, anxieties, doubts, vulnerability, PIN number, passwords, etc. How many people in your life do you trust with absolutely anything and everything? How many people do you know *everything* about? Probably not a ton.

Trust is a key component in our relationship with God and with one another. If we do not trust God, our faith will ultimately be in ourselves, which is a dead end (literally). If we do not trust others, our existence will become self-focused and empty. Today's gospel is a great example of what happens when God trusts us but we don't trust in him or in the abilities he has given to us. The failure to act on the part of the person with one talent demonstrated a lack of trust and a sin of omission (which you can read more about in the Behind the Scenes section). Our faithfulness demonstrates a trust in God, and our foolishness denotes a lack of trust in God and in the abilities and talents (no pun intended) that he's entrusted to us.

The righteous woman depicted in Proverbs is the one who her husband can trust completely: her grace-filled and Spirit-led life, her consistent trust in God, and her own trustworthiness. Likewise, the good friends seen in the second reading—the "children of the light"—are faithful and solid and can be counted upon at all times. This consistency and steadiness shown in both the first and second reading becomes, then, an example of the types of souls we must become and the way we are to live at all times. Sooner or later the Lord is coming back, and the ones who will be chosen (and not cast into the darkness) are the ones who "knew the Master" well enough to trust him in all manners and to be confident in the skills and blessings entrusted to them for his glory.

RELATED FACT

The "talent" described in the gospel was worth money but was not exactly "currency." Much like gold or silver can be bought and sold and are worth a good amount, talents were ancient units of weight made of precious metals. The more valuable the metal (e.g., gold versus copper) and the heavier, the greater the worth.

BEHIND THE SCENES

As explained above, it is impossible to put an exact price or value on a biblical talent; suffice to say, entrusting even one would have been bold on the master's part. The "journey" alluded to in this parable can be seen as a representation of the time between Jesus's Ascension and the judgment upon Jerusalem (AD 70). In that time, the disciples were given the Holy Spirit, others came to know the Lord through his Church, and still others heard the message loosely passed along by eyewitnesses. The point is that everyone had been "given" something from the Master to work with. We see in the servant given only one talent the fear and unwillingness to do anything with what was entrusted to him (which was still a very valuable thing). The servant is not only deemed lazy but "wicked"! Some scholars have even argued that it was precisely *because* the master only trusted this servant with the one talent that the servant purposefully buried it so the master would be assured of no interest and, thus, no profit as a way of retribution.

Put into a modern, spiritual context, the analogy offers us an invaluable lesson. We can extend this premise to actual talents and skills or even spiritual gifts that we have as modern disciples. We see very clearly what the Lord's hopes and expectations are for us. Heaven expects Earth to act. God desires for his children to use everything at their disposal to help return to him that which he values most—souls. Not only are we to live our lives with humble boldness, as evidenced by how we use the talents entrusted to us, but our lives ought to be so boldly beautiful that others are attracted to them. We must take full advantage of the time and talents we have to touch as many souls as possible for God.

A closer examination of the gospels reveals an intriguing trend with the Lord, too. Consider the sins of commission we hear about (e.g., the woman caught in adultery, the good thief on the cross) and how merciful the Lord is with each soul. Look, then, at the sins of omission (e.g., the other nine disciples unable or unwilling to heal, the Pharisees who neglect hospitality, etc.) and how sternly the Lord rebukes his followers when they should have acted but did not.

WORD PLAY

The first reading makes mention of the righteous woman working with a *distaff*. A distaff is a tool (often looking like a stick) used to hold unspun fibers (like flax or wool) and keep them free of tangles while the spinning process is happening. It's a precursor to the spindle.

JOURNAL

1. Are you trustworthy? Why or why not? Be honest.
2. Is there a friend in your life who is trustworthy? How does he or she demonstrate that trustworthiness?

3. What makes it difficult to trust in a friend? What makes it difficult to trust in God?

4. Is there a particular gift God has given you that you are called to use for his glory alone? How well are you using that gift? What, if anything, is holding you back?

CHALLENGE FOR THE WEEK

Find some time to talk to someone you really trust (see Journal question 2) about the area you meditated upon in the Opening Prayer. Ask that person to pray for you and this intention, specifically, this next week; and in any moment that you are feeling anxious, pray those five simple words, "Jesus, I trust in you."

His Glorious Throne

Solemnity of Christ the King

OPENING PRAYER

Lord God, King of my heart, someday you will come in your glory to separate the sheep from the goats. If you come while I am still on this Earth, may I be put on your right side. Teach me, today, what it is that I need to do to ensure a life forever in your heavenly kingdom. Amen.

> **First Reading:** Ezekiel 34:11–12, 15–17
> **Responsorial Psalm:** Psalm 23:1–6
> **Second Reading:** 1 Corinthians 15:20–26, 28
> **Gospel:** Matthew 25:31–46

BEYOND WORDS

The past few weeks you have probably noticed a "shift" in the tone and content of the Sunday readings, in particular the gospels. As we've spoken about previously, the imagery has grown quite stark, and the context of the readings has dealt a great deal with the coming last judgment. As we close this liturgical year, today's readings crescendo with this parable that so strongly urges us all to be living rightly—for the Son of Man is, indeed, coming to survey and "repay" everyone according to their conduct.

We see Christ the King coming with the angels but in the role of a shepherd-king, who separates sheep (the righteous ones) from goats. The separation is based not on our intentions but on our actions. How often or seldom have we served another in the name of Christ? Do we seek to serve "kings" (popular) but forget the lowly (unpopular)? It is by our actions toward God and others that our true nature—and our true "king"—is revealed. A shepherd, though having authority over his sheep, demonstrates his great love by serving them and risking his life for them.

This is an extension of the Good Shepherd imagery employed by the prophet Ezekiel in the first reading. We see God as proactively seeking out the lost sheep, even before any judgment or separation. We are given every opportunity to be in the Lord's sheepfold. God is proactive, which is a theme we see put forth to the Corinthians. God did not leave us in our death but, rather, pursued and ransomed us through his only Son. He is the shepherd who not only seeks out the lost sheep but sacrifices his life for them. He is a servant-king, humble in his great power and unyielding in his pursuit and protection of us. His greatness was veiled as meekness on Earth but reveals the power of his great glory—for the Shepherd became the Lamb, and the Lamb sits on the throne forever and ever. Amen.

RELATED FACT

We hear a lot of imagery involving sheep and shepherds this week. The bishop is considered the shepherd of his diocese, which is why he carries his hooked "shepherd's staff" called a *crozier*.

BEHIND THE SCENES

Have you ever noticed the preference given to "the right hand" in scripture? Where do we proclaim that Christ is seated in heaven? He is seated at the right hand of the Father.

In the ancient world, the right hand or side was always associated with good fortune and honor, while the left hand or side was normally viewed through a less fortunate, dishonorable lens. Some scholars have suggested that this had to do with something as simple as etiquette when going to the bathroom (although they had no formal "bathroom," obviously). The left hand was known as the hand used to wipe after defecation, making it less preferable.

Note that, in this parable, strong preference is given to the sheep and those sheep are placed at the Good Shepherd's right, while the goats will be dismissed out to his left.

WORD PLAY

The word *crozier* (as referenced in the Related Fact above) comes from *croisier*, which is French for "cross bearer."

JOURNAL

1. When was the last time you served the "least of these" (Mt 25:45): the poor, hungry, thirsty, naked, imprisoned, and so on? What was the experience like?

2. Is it ever difficult for you to serve the marginalized? Why or why not?

3. If God were to come again today, what would he say to you?

CHALLENGE FOR THE WEEK

Serving the "least of these" doesn't always look like what we think it should. Sometimes, it may mean serving those we struggle with at work, or it may mean small acts of kindness for those close to you who are having a bad day. This week, pray for the ability to see those who need God's love. Additionally, pray for the ability to see how it is he is calling you to love those people. Then act upon those moments with the confidence that God is with you.

Mark Hart—also known as the "Bible Geek"—is the chief innovation officer at Life Teen International. He is an award-winning producer of Bible study DVDs and the author of more than twenty books, including the bestselling and award-winning *Blessed Are the Bored in Spirit*. He is the coauthor—with his wife, Melanie—of *Our Not-Quite-Holy Family, Embracing God's Plan for Marriage*, and *Getting More Out of Marriage*.

A graduate of the University of Notre Dame, Hart is a blogger, podcaster, and international speaker. He is a research fellow at the St. Paul Center for Biblical Theology.

He lives in the Phoenix, Arizona, area with his family.

Biblegeek.com
Facebook: @MarkHart99
Twitter: @LT_thebiblegeek
Instagram: @biblegeek

AVE

AVE MARIA PRESS

Founded in 1865, Ave Maria Press,
a ministry of the Congregation of
Holy Cross, is a Catholic publishing
company that serves the spiritual and
formative needs of the Church and its
schools, institutions, and ministers;
Christian individuals and families; and
others seeking spiritual nourishment.

For a complete listing of titles from

Ave Maria Press

Sorin Books

Forest of Peace

Christian Classics

visit www.avemariapress.com

AVE MARIA PRESS
Notre Dame, IN
A Ministry of the United States Province of Holy Cross